P9-CAU-374

Quick & Healthy
SPIRALIZED

pil

Publications International, Ltd.

Copyright © 2016 Publications International, Ltd.
All rights reserved. This publication may not be reproduced or quoted in whole or in part by any means whatsoever without written permission from:

Louis Weber, CEO
Publications International, Ltd.
8140 Lehigh Ave
Morton Grove, IL 60053

Permission is never granted for commercial purposes.

Photography on pages 4, 6, 13, 22, 33, 38, 42, 45, 48, 54, 57, 58, 67, 68, 71, 72, 75, 76, 81, 82, 85, 89, 90, 93, 96, 99, 105, 106, 112, 116, 119, 125, 126, 129, 130, 133, 134, 138, 141, 142 and 151 by PIL Photo Studio.

All recipes and recipe photographs copyright © Publications International, Ltd.

Pictured on the front cover: Zoodles in Tomato Sauce *(page 111)*.

Pictured on the back cover *(clockwise from top left):* Roasted Curly Carrots, Potatoes and Onions *(page 139)*, Farmers' Market Potato Salad *(page 56)*, Zucchini and Sweet Potato Stuffed Peppers *(page 140)* and Pasta Primavera with Ricotta *(page 124)*.

ISBN: 978-1-68022-312-5

Library of Congress Control Number: 2015956147

Manufactured in China.

8 7 6 5 4 3 2 1

Nutritional Analysis: Every effort has been made to check the accuracy of the nutritional information that appears with each recipe. However, because numerous variables account for a wide range of values for certain foods, nutritive analyses in this book should be considered approximate. Different results may be obtained by using different nutrient databases and different brand-name products.

Microwave Cooking: Microwave ovens vary in wattage. Use the cooking times as guidelines and check for doneness before adding more time.

Note: This publication is only intended to provide general information. The information is specifically not intended to be a substitute for medical diagnosis or treatment by your physician or other health care professional. You should always consult your own physician or other health care professionals about any medical questions, diagnosis, or treatment. (Products vary among manufacturers. Please check labels carefully to confirm nutritional values.)

The information obtained by you from this book should not be relied upon for any personal, nutritional, or medical decision. You should consult an appropriate professional for specific advice tailored to your specific situation. PIL makes no representations or warranties, express or implied, with respect to your use of this information.

In no event shall PIL, its affiliates or advertisers be liable for any direct, indirect, punitive, incidental, special, or consequential damages, or any damages whatsoever including, without limitation, damages for personal injury, death, damage to property, or loss of profits, arising out of or in any way connected with the use of any of the above-referenced information or otherwise arising out of the use of this book.

Publications International, Ltd.

Table of Contents

Welcome to the world of spiralizing! Here are some general tips and notes on specific vegetables to get you started.

GENERAL TIPS

• Choose firm vegetables without any soft spots. Too-soft produce and mushy spots don't spiralize well.

• Secure the wider end of the item onto your spiralizer's support spikes. Make sure it is firmly attached or it may come loose and fall off during spiralizing.

• For perfect half-moon slices, spiral your fruit or vegetable with the spiral slicing blade. Stand it on a cutting board and cut it in half vertically. For smaller quarter slices, make two vertical perpendicular cuts through the top.

• Many vegetables will be too long to use right after spiralizing, so you'll need to trim them. Pick up bunches of spirals and cut them into desired lengths with kitchen shears, or pile them on a cutting board and make a few cuts to shorten the pieces a bit. For significant shortening, coarsely chop them.

SPIRALIZING BLADES

Your spiralizer likely came with a minimum of the following three standard blades.

Thin ribbon blade: This blade has small triangle-shaped teeth that cut vegetables into long, thin ribbons. Use this blade when replacing pasta with vegetables or when you need the vegetables to cook faster.

Thick ribbon blade: This blade has larger triangle-shaped teeth that cut vegetables into long ribbons that are thicker than the thin blade.

Spiral slicing blade: This straight blade cuts vegetables into a long continuous slice. Use it to make hasselback potatoes or apples; for slicing bell peppers; or to make half-moon slices.

Thin ribbon blade

Thick ribbon blade

Spiral slicing blade

VEGETABLES AND FRUIT

Apples and Pears: Although apples and pears work perfectly well with the ribbon blades, you'll probably use the spiral slicing blade most often. Slices of apples and pears tend to be more useful than ribbons, although ribbons do make a fun snack that kids love.

Beets: You can peel beets before spiralizing them, or just scrub them well to remove dirt and debris and spiral them with the skin on. Beet skin is usually thin and won't be noticeable in the spirals. Be aware that the juice of red beets tends to mist a bit during spiralizing, so protect your clothing and work space.

Bell Peppers: Bell peppers and poblano peppers spiral surprisingly well (although occasionally a pepper will come along that does not want to be spiraled; you'll just have to slice it with a knife). Remove the stem, leaving the stem end intact; secure this end onto the support spikes. Cut the pepper with the spiral slicing blade to make one long, thin slice.

Butternut Squash: Peel the whole butternut squash, cut it in half and then work with it in two parts. The neck spiralizes into ribbons and spiral slices well; simply cut it into 3-inch pieces and spiral as usual. The bulb, however, needs a bit of work. Cut it in half and scoop out the seeds, forming two cuplike shapes. Secure the widest part of the squash against the support spikes and then slowly and carefully spiral the squash. It may fall off; reposition and try again until it is fully spiraled.

Carrots: Choose large carrots (sometimes called "soup carrots") about 1½ to 2 inches in diameter for spiralizing into ribbons. Small carrots can spiral, but they tend to split apart and crumble.

Cucumbers: Seedless cucumbers are neater to spiral, although regular cucumbers work equally well; you'll just have some seeds to pick out of the spirals. All three blades work well on cucumbers.

Leeks: Cut off the root end and trim off the top leaves at the point where the green part becomes darker and less tightly wrapped. The spiral slicing blade works best on leeks (the ribbon blades tend to tear them up too much).

Onions: Onions were made to be spiralized. Because of their layers, they look the same with all three blades, the only difference being the thickness of the slice. The spiral slicing blade produces the thickest spirals, while the thin and thick ribbon blades produce fine and medium spirals. When a recipe calls for half of an onion, cut it in half crosswise (through the equator) and secure the cut end onto the support spikes.

Potatoes and Sweet Potatoes:
Cut potatoes into 3-inch pieces
if you're making ribbons; if you're
using the spiral slicing blade, keep
them whole (whole spiral sliced
potatoes make great hasselback
potatoes). All types of potatoes
work well with all three blades.

Radishes: Larger radishes like
daikon, black and watermelon work
best, although small red radishes
will spiral with any of the blades.

Zucchini and Yellow Squash: In this
book, a small zucchini is about
6 ounces, a medium is 8 to
10 ounces and a large is 12 ounces
or more. When replacing pasta
with zucchini noodles ("zoodles"),
figure about 8 ounces of zucchini
per serving. Cut the squash into
approximately 3-inch pieces; this
way your ribbons won't be too long
and you'll have more control when
spiralizing. Both vegetables work
well with all three blades.

**Other vegetables that can be
successfully spiralized include:**
jicama, turnips, rutabaga, kohlrabi,
cabbage and parsnips.

KEY TO THE ICONS
Recipes are marked with icons
indicating various health attributes.

GF GLUTEN-FREE
*Recipes do not contain any gluten,
but check ingredient lists of packaged
foods to make sure you're using gluten-
free products.*

DF DAIRY-FREE
*Recipes do not contain any dairy
products.*

V VEGETARIAN
*Recipes do not contain any meat or
meat broth, although they may contain
cheese or eggs.*

V+ VEGAN
*Recipes do not contain any dairy, eggs,
meat or other animal products.*

LC LOW-CARB
*Recipes contain 15 grams or less of
carbohydrate per serving.*

LS LOW-SODIUM
*Recipes have 140 milligrams of
sodium or less per serving.*

HF HIGH-FIBER
*Recipes contain 5 grams of fiber or
more per serving.*

Spiral sliced green pepper

Spiral sliced pear

Spiralized zucchini "zoodles"

Breakfast

BUCKWHEAT BREAKFAST BOWL

Buckwheat is popular around the world, especially in Asia and Eastern Europe (think Japanese soba noodles and Russian blini), both in kernel and flour form. Despite its name, buckwheat has no relation to wheat and is, in fact, not even a grain (it's related to rhubarb), making it safe for gluten-free diets. This recipe uses kasha, the toasted hulled, crushed kernels of the buckwheat plant; it has a toasted, nutty flavor that pairs well with cinnamon, maple syrup, vanilla and sautéed apples. If you can't find kasha with the grains at the grocery store, try the kosher section.

3 to 4 cups reduced-fat (2%) milk*

2 tablespoons packed brown sugar

½ teaspoon vanilla

½ teaspoon ground cinnamon, divided

1 cup kasha

2 apples

2 teaspoons butter

¼ cup chopped walnuts

2 tablespoons maple syrup

For a creamier consistency, use more milk.

1. Combine milk, brown sugar, vanilla and ¼ teaspoon cinnamon in large saucepan. Bring to a boil over medium heat. Stir in kasha; reduce heat to low. Cook and stir 8 to 10 minutes or until kasha is tender and liquid is absorbed.

2. Meanwhile, spiral apples with thick ribbon blade; coarsely chop (1- to 2-inch pieces work best).

3. Melt butter in large nonstick skillet over medium heat. Stir in remaining ¼ teaspoon cinnamon. Add apples; cook and stir 4 to 5 minutes or until tender. Stir in walnuts and maple syrup; heat through.

4. Divide kasha among serving bowls; top with apple mixture. Serve immediately.

Makes 6 servings

Calories 226, **Total Fat** 8g, **Saturated Fat** 3g, **Cholesterol** 13mg, **Sodium** 119mg, **Carbohydrate** 34g, **Dietary Fiber** 3g, **Protein** 6g

APPLE AND RAISIN OVEN PANCAKE

This custardy apple pancake comes together quickly with your spiralizer handling the apple prep; you'll have perfect apple slices in seconds. Honeycrisp, Granny Smith, Gala and Braeburn are all good choices for this recipe.

1 large apple

⅓ cup golden raisins

2 tablespoons packed brown sugar

½ teaspoon ground cinnamon

4 eggs

⅔ cup milk

⅔ cup all-purpose flour

2 tablespoons butter, melted

1. Preheat oven to 350°F. Spray 9-inch pie plate with nonstick cooking spray.

2. Spiral apple with spiral slicing blade. Stand apple on cutting board and cut in half to make slices.

3. Combine apple, raisins, brown sugar and cinnamon in medium bowl. Arrange in prepared pie plate.

4. Bake 10 to 15 minutes or until apple begins to soften. Remove from oven. *Increase oven temperature to 450°F.*

5. Meanwhile, whisk eggs, milk, flour and butter in medium bowl until blended. Pour batter over apple mixture.

6. Bake 15 minutes or until pancake is golden brown. Cut into wedges to serve.

Makes 6 servings

Calories 202, **Total Fat** 8g, **Saturated Fat** 4g, **Cholesterol** 153mg, **Sodium** 89mg, **Carbohydrate** 27g, **Dietary Fiber** 1g, **Protein** 7g

SWEET POTATO AND TURKEY SAUSAGE HASH GF DF

Rethink hash with this colorful version that brings a bit of fun to the breakfast table. Ribbons of colorful vegetables and sweet potatoes replace regular potatoes, and turkey sausage shows its playful side when shaped into tiny meatballs. For hash in a hurry, skip the meatball step; remove sausage from the casings and cook as directed in step 2, breaking up sausage into bite-size pieces with a wooden spoon.

1 red onion

1 sweet potato, peeled

1 red bell pepper

2 mild or hot turkey Italian sausage links (about 4 ounces each)

½ teaspoon salt

¼ teaspoon black pepper

⅛ teaspoon ground cumin

⅛ teaspoon chipotle chili powder

1. Spiral onion with thin ribbon blade. Spiral sweet potato with thick ribbon blade. Spiral bell pepper with spiral slicing blade. Cut vegetables into desired lengths.

2. Remove sausage from casings; shape sausage into ½-inch balls. Spray large nonstick skillet with nonstick cooking spray; heat over medium heat. Add sausage; cook and stir 3 to 5 minutes or until browned. Remove from skillet; set aside.

3. Spray same skillet with cooking spray. Add onion, sweet potato, bell pepper, salt, black pepper, cumin and chili powder; cook and stir 5 to 8 minutes or until sweet potato is tender.

4. Stir in sausage; cook without stirring 5 minutes or until hash is lightly browned on bottom.

Makes 2 to 4 servings

Calories 270, **Total Fat** 12g, **Saturated Fat** 0g, **Cholesterol** 17mg, **Sodium** 770mg, **Carbohydrate** 19g, **Dietary Fiber** 4g, **Protein** 21g

ZUCCHINI-DATE BREAD · V

For the best distribution of zucchini throughout this bread, coarsely chop the zucchini into 1-inch (or smaller) pieces. Also, it will retain some of its shape during baking and smaller pieces are easier to slice and eat.

BREAD

- 1 cup chopped pitted dates
- 1 cup water
- 1 small zucchini
- 1 cup whole wheat flour
- 1 cup all-purpose flour
- 2 tablespoons granulated sugar
- 1 teaspoon baking powder
- ½ teaspoon baking soda
- ½ teaspoon salt
- ½ teaspoon ground cinnamon
- ¼ teaspoon ground cloves
- 2 eggs

CREAM CHEESE SPREAD

- 1 package (8 ounces) fat-free cream cheese, softened
- ¼ cup powdered sugar
- 1 tablespoon vanilla
- ⅛ teaspoon ground cinnamon

1. Preheat oven to 350°F. Spray 8×4-inch loaf pan with nonstick cooking spray.

2. Combine dates and water in small saucepan; bring to a boil over medium-high heat. Remove from heat; let stand 15 minutes. Spiral zucchini with thin ribbon blade; coarsely chop.

3. Combine flours, granulated sugar, baking powder, baking soda, salt, ½ teaspoon cinnamon and cloves in large bowl.

4. Whisk eggs in medium bowl; stir in date mixture and zucchini. Stir egg mixture into flour mixture just until moistened. Pour into prepared pan.

5. Bake 30 to 35 minutes or until toothpick inserted into center comes out clean. Cool 5 minutes. Remove to wire rack; cool completely.

6. Meanwhile, prepare cream cheese spread. Beat cream cheese, powdered sugar, vanilla and ⅛ teaspoon cinnamon in small bowl until smooth and well blended. Cover and refrigerate until ready to use.

7. Cut bread into 16 slices. Serve with cream cheese spread.

Makes 16 servings

....

Calories 124, **Total Fat** 1g, **Saturated Fat** 1g, **Cholesterol** 27mg, **Sodium** 260mg, **Carbohydrate** 24g, **Dietary Fiber** 2g, **Protein** 5g

....

WARM APPLE AND BLUEBERRY CRISP

Although generally found among the desserts, crisps make a delightful breakfast when served alongside Greek yogurt. To make this crisp for dessert, add an additional 2 tablespoons brown sugar to the fruit mixture in step 3 and serve with vanilla frozen yogurt or ice cream.

6 apples, peeled

2 cups frozen blueberries

¼ cup plus 2 tablespoons packed brown sugar, divided

¼ cup orange juice

½ cup biscuit baking mix

½ cup old-fashioned oats

¼ cup (½ stick) cold butter, cut into small pieces

¼ teaspoon ground cinnamon

¼ teaspoon ground ginger

1. Preheat oven to 375°F. Spray 9-inch square baking pan with nonstick cooking spray.

2. Spiral apples with spiral slicing blade. Stand apples on cutting board and cut in half to make slices.

3. Combine apples, blueberries, 2 tablespoons brown sugar and orange juice in medium bowl; toss to coat. Spoon into prepared pan.

4. Combine baking mix, oats, remaining ¼ cup brown sugar, butter, cinnamon and ginger in small bowl; mix with fingers until coarse crumbs form. Sprinkle over fruit mixture.

5. Bake 45 minutes or until apples are tender and topping is golden brown.

Makes 8 servings

Calories 220, **Total Fat** 8g, **Saturated Fat** 4g, **Cholesterol** 15mg, **Sodium** 270mg, **Carbohydrate** 38g, **Dietary Fiber** 3g, **Protein** 2g

HAM AND SWISS POTATO RÖSTI

Rösti potatoes, Switzerland's answer to potato pancakes, are usually served as a side dish at breakfast but they often make an appearance at other meals as well. Packed with cheese, ham and spinach, this version can stand on its own, or top it with a poached egg for a heartier meal.

1 small onion

3 to 4 red potatoes, peeled

5 teaspoons olive oil, divided

¾ cup (3 ounces) shredded Swiss cheese, divided

⅓ cup thawed frozen spinach, pressed dry

1 ounce low-sodium ham, diced

2 egg whites, lightly beaten

1. Spiral onion with thin ribbon blade; cut into desired lengths. Spiral potatoes with thin ribbon blade; coarsely chop and measure 3 cups. Press dry with paper towels.

2. Heat 1 teaspoon oil in medium nonstick skillet over medium heat. Add onion; cook and stir 5 minutes or until tender. Transfer to large bowl. Add potatoes, ½ cup cheese, spinach, ham and egg whites; gently mix.

3. Wipe out skillet with paper towels. Heat 2 teaspoons oil over medium heat. Add potato mixture, pressing down lightly into skillet to form flat layer. Cook 5 minutes, lifting edges to allow uncooked portion to flow underneath.

4. Place large plate over skillet. Invert rösti onto plate. Wipe out skillet with paper towels.

5. Heat remaining 2 teaspoons oil over medium heat. Return rösti, uncooked side down, to skillet. Sprinkle with remaining ¼ cup cheese. Cook 5 minutes or until browned and cheese is melted. Let stand 5 minutes before cutting.

Makes 6 servings

Calories 196, **Total Fat** 9g, **Saturated Fat** 3g, **Cholesterol** 15mg, **Sodium** 117mg, **Carbohydrate** 21g, **Dietary Fiber** 2g, **Protein** 9g

APPLE-CRANBERRY NOODLE KUGEL

Kugel is a versatile dish that is just as comfortable as a breakfast as it is a side dish or dessert, and is open to customization. Swap raisins, chopped dried dates or apricots for the cranberries, try brown sugar instead of the granulated sugar, or give it a crunchy topping (crushed flaky cereal or bread crumbs mixed with a bit of melted butter).

8 ounces uncooked egg noodles

2 apples

1 cup dried cranberries

3 eggs

¾ cup sugar

1 cup reduced-fat sour cream

1 cup cottage cheese

1 teaspoon vanilla

¼ teaspoon ground cinnamon

1. Preheat oven to 350°F. Lightly coat 8-inch square baking dish with nonstick cooking spray. Cook noodles according to package directions. Drain and rinse under cold water; return to saucepan.

2. Spiral apples with spiral slicing blade. Stand on cutting board and cut in half to make slices. Add to noodles with cranberries; mix well.

3. Whisk eggs and sugar in large bowl until thick and pale yellow. Whisk in sour cream, cottage cheese, vanilla and cinnamon. Pour over noodle mixture; stir until well blended. Spread in prepared baking dish.

4. Cover baking dish with foil. Bake 55 minutes or just until set.

Makes 8 servings

Calories 350, **Total Fat** 8g, **Saturated Fat** 4g, **Cholesterol** 125mg, **Sodium** 150mg, **Carbohydrate** 63g, **Dietary Fiber** 3g, **Protein** 11g

Appetizers & Snacks

CURLY CURRY CHIPS · Ⓥ

Curry chips are a favorite pub snack and street food in England and Ireland. This version swaps thick, heavy chips for lighter-than-air baked curly potatoes and pairs them with a super simple curry dipping sauce.

- 4 small *or* 2 large russet potatoes, peeled
- 1 teaspoon vegetable oil
- ¾ teaspoon salt, divided
- 1 tablespoon butter
- ¼ cup finely chopped onion
- 1 tablespoon all-purpose flour
- 1 tablespoon curry powder
- 1 cup reduced-sodium vegetable broth

1. Preheat oven to 450°F. Line large baking sheet with parchment paper.

2. Spiral potatoes with thick ribbon blade; cut into desired lengths. Spread potatoes on prepared baking sheet; drizzle with oil. Bake 30 to 35 minutes or until golden brown and crispy, turning once. Sprinkle with ½ teaspoon salt.

3. Melt butter in small saucepan over medium-high heat. Add onion; cook and stir about 3 minutes or until softened. Whisk in flour and curry powder until well blended; cook 1 minute, stirring constantly. Add vegetable broth in thin steady stream, whisking constantly.

4. Reduce heat to medium. Cook about 10 minutes or until thick. Taste and add additional ¼ teaspoon salt, if desired. For smooth sauce, cool slightly and purée in blender or food processor. Serve with potatoes.

Makes 4 servings

Calories 180, **Total Fat** 4.5g, **Saturated Fat** 2g, **Cholesterol** 10mg, **Sodium** 500mg, **Carbohydrate** 32g, **Dietary Fiber** 4g, **Protein** 4g

GOAT CHEESE, CARAMELIZED ONION AND PROSCIUTTO FLATBREAD

This flatbread makes a great lunch or light dinner; just add a simple salad to make it a meal. For added texture and sweetness, try sprinkling a handful of halved red grapes over the goat cheese before baking.

1 large onion
2 tablespoons olive oil
¼ teaspoon salt
¼ cup water
1 package (about 14 ounces) refrigerated pizza dough
2 ounces crumbled goat cheese
4 slices prosciutto
½ teaspoon fresh thyme leaves

1. Preheat oven to 450°F. Line baking sheet with parchment paper.

2. Spiral onion with thick ribbon blade or spiral slicing blade; cut into desired lengths.

3. Heat oil in large skillet over medium heat. Add onion and salt; cook about 18 to 20 minutes or until onion is golden brown, stirring occasionally and adding water halfway through cooking.

4. Divide pizza dough in half. Roll each half into 9×5-inch rectangle on lightly floured surface; transfer dough to prepared baking sheet. Top evenly with onions, goat cheese and prosciutto.

5. Bake 12 minutes or until crust is golden brown and prosciutto is crisp. Sprinkle with thyme. Cut each flatbread into 6 pieces.

Makes 12 servings

Calories 130, **Total Fat** 5g, **Saturated Fat** 2g, **Cholesterol** 10mg, **Sodium** 440mg, **Carbohydrate** 17g, **Dietary Fiber** 1g, **Protein** 5g

RHUBARB CHUTNEY

Try this sweet-tart chutney on crackers with a sharp aged Cheddar. Or spread it over a wheel of brie or a block of cream cheese and bake until the cheese is soft. It's also great as an accompaniment to roast pork or ham.

1 apple

½ cup sugar

¼ cup water

¼ cup dark raisins

1 teaspoon grated lemon peel

2 cups sliced rhubarb (½-inch pieces)

3 tablespoons coarsely chopped pecans

2 to 3 teaspoons white vinegar

¾ teaspoon ground cinnamon (optional)

Assorted crackers and cheese (optional)

1. Spiral apple with spiral slicing blade. Stand on cutting board and cut into quarters.

2. Combine apple, sugar, water, raisins and lemon peel in medium saucepan; cook over medium heat until sugar is dissolved, stirring constantly. Reduce heat to low; simmer, uncovered, about 5 minutes or until apple is almost tender.

3. Stir in rhubarb and pecans; bring to a boil over high heat. Reduce heat to low; simmer 8 to 10 minutes or until slightly thickened and rhubarb is tender, stirring occasionally. Stir in vinegar and cinnamon, if desired, during last 2 to 3 minutes of cooking.

4. Remove from heat; cool to room temperature. Cover and refrigerate until ready to serve. Serve with crackers and cheese, if desired.

Makes 16 servings (about 2 cups)

Calories 91, **Total Fat** 2g, **Saturated Fat** 1g, **Cholesterol** 0mg, **Sodium** 2mg, **Carbohydrate** 20g, **Dietary Fiber** 1g, **Protein** 1g

KALE, MUSHROOM AND ONION PIZZA

Your spiralizer can transform an onion into a pile of perfectly uniform slices in a matter of seconds. Throw the whole pile in the skillet as-is (the onions will shrink dramatically) or cut them into small pieces. Mound them on a cutting board and make two perpendicular cuts all the way through.

1 package (about 14 ounces) refrigerated pizza dough

1 yellow onion

1 tablespoon olive oil

1 package (8 ounces) sliced mushrooms

3 cloves garlic, minced

4 cups packed coarsely chopped kale

¼ teaspoon red pepper flakes

½ cup pizza sauce

¾ cup (3 ounces) finely shredded part-skim mozzarella cheese

1. Preheat oven to 425°F. Spray 15×10-inch jelly-roll pan with nonstick cooking spray. Unroll pizza dough on prepared pan. Press dough evenly into pan and ½ inch up sides. Prick dough all over with fork. Bake 7 to 10 minutes or until lightly browned.

2. Spiral onion with thick ribbon blade or spiral slicing blade; cut into desired lengths.

3. Heat oil in large nonstick skillet over medium heat. Add onion; cook and stir 15 minutes or until golden brown. Add mushrooms and garlic; cook and stir 4 minutes. Add kale and red pepper flakes; cover and cook 2 minutes to wilt kale. Uncover; cook and stir 3 to 4 minutes or until vegetables are tender.

4. Spread pizza sauce over crust. Spread kale mixture evenly over sauce; top with cheese. Bake 10 minutes or until crust is golden brown.

Makes 12 servings

Calories 130, **Total Fat** 4g, **Saturated Fat** 2g, **Cholesterol** 5mg, **Sodium** 350mg, **Carbohydrate** 19g, **Dietary Fiber** 1g, **Protein** 5g

SPANISH POTATO OMELET GF DF V LC

Think of this omelet as mini quiche without the crust; cut it into cubes for a party snack or into wedges for smaller gatherings. Serve with marcona almonds, Manchego cheese and toasted French bread slices.

1 pound unpeeled red or white potatoes

½ green bell pepper

½ red bell pepper

1 small onion

2 teaspoons olive oil

2 teaspoons vegetable oil

½ teaspoon salt, divided

3 eggs

½ teaspoon paprika

1. Spiral potatoes with spiral slicing blade; stand on cutting board and cut in half to make slices. Spiral bell peppers and onion with spiral slicing blade; cut into desired lengths.

2. Heat oils in large skillet over medium-high heat. Add potatoes; sprinkle with ¼ teaspoon salt and stir to coat with oil. Cook 6 to 9 minutes or until potatoes are translucent, stirring occasionally.

3. Add bell peppers and onion. Reduce heat to medium. Cook 10 minutes or until potatoes are tender, turning occasionally. Drain mixture in colander set over large bowl; reserve oil. Let potato mixture stand until cool.

4. Beat eggs, paprika and remaining ¼ teaspoon salt in separate large bowl. Gently stir in potato mixture until coated. Let stand 15 minutes.

5. Heat 2 teaspoons reserved oil in small nonstick skillet over medium-high heat. Add potato mixture; spread in even layer. Cook until bottom and side are set and top still looks moist. Flip omelet onto large plate, then slide back into skillet. Continue to cook until bottom is lightly browned. Slide omelet onto serving plate. Let stand 30 minutes before serving. Cut into wedges.

Makes 8 servings

Calories 90, **Total Fat** 4g, **Saturated Fat** 1g, **Cholesterol** 70mg, **Sodium** 180mg, **Carbohydrate** 11g, **Dietary Fiber** 2g, **Protein** 4g

MUSHROOM AND ZUCCHINI QUESADILLAS (V) (HF)

1 onion

1 small zucchini

1 portobello mushroom, sliced

¾ cup (3 ounces) reduced-fat shredded Colby and Monterey Jack cheese

4 (6-inch) whole wheat tortillas

½ cup salsa

1. Spiral onion and zucchini with thin ribbon blade; cut into desired lengths.

2. Spray large nonstick skillet with nonstick cooking spray; heat over medium-high heat. Add onion, zucchini and mushroom; cook 4 minutes, stirring frequently.

3. Spoon one fourth of cheese and one fourth of vegetable mixture onto one half of each tortilla. Fold tortillas in half.

4. Spray skillet with cooking spray; heat over medium heat. Cook tortillas in batches 2 minutes per side or until lightly browned on both sides. Cut tortillas in half and serve with salsa.

Makes 4 servings

Calories 213, **Total Fat** 8g, **Saturated Fat** 3g, **Cholesterol** 15mg, **Sodium** 530mg, **Carbohydrate** 26g, **Dietary Fiber** 5g, **Protein** 11g

BUTTERNUT SQUASH OVEN CHIPS

For a sweet snack, substitute cinnamon or pumpkin pie spice for the garlic powder. In the dip, omit the mayonnaise and increase the yogurt to ½ cup. Stir in 1 tablespoon packed dark brown sugar.

Lime Yogurt Dip
(recipe follows)

½ teaspoon garlic powder

¼ teaspoon salt

¼ teaspoon ground red pepper

1 butternut squash (about 2½ pounds), peeled and seeded

2 teaspoons vegetable oil

1. Preheat oven to 425°F. Prepare Lime Yogurt Dip. Combine garlic powder, salt and ground red pepper in small bowl.

2. Spiral butternut squash with spiral slicing blade. Stand on cutting board and cut in half to make slices. Spread squash on baking sheet. Drizzle with oil and sprinkle with seasoning mix; gently toss to coat. Arrange in single layer.

3. Bake 20 to 25 minutes or until squash is browned and crisp, turning occasionally.

Makes 4 servings

Lime Yogurt Dip: Combine ¼ cup reduced-fat mayonnaise, ¼ cup reduced-fat Greek yogurt, 1 teaspoon lime juice and ¼ teaspoon grated lime peel in small bowl. Refrigerate until ready to serve.

Calories 190, **Total Fat** 8g, **Saturated Fat** 1g, **Cholesterol** 5mg, **Sodium** 260mg, **Carbohydrate** 32g, **Dietary Fiber** 5g, **Protein** 4g

ROSEMARY AND ONION FOCACCIA

Focaccia is as easy to customize as pizza. For variations, try swapping out the rosemary and fontina for the following combinations: thyme and Asiago; pesto sauce and fresh mozzarella; or roasted red peppers and Gruyère.

1 loaf (16 ounces) frozen bread dough, thawed

4 onions

1 tablespoon olive oil

½ teaspoon salt

2 tablespoons water

1 tablespoon chopped fresh rosemary

¼ teaspoon black pepper

½ cup (2 ounces) shredded fontina cheese

¼ cup grated Parmesan cheese

1. Spray 13×9-inch baking pan with nonstick cooking spray. Roll out dough into 13×9-inch rectangle on lightly floured surface; place in prepared pan. Cover and let rise in warm place 30 minutes.

2. Spiral onions with thick ribbon blade or spiral slicing blade; cut into desired lengths.

3. Heat oil in large skillet over medium-high heat. Add onions and salt; cook 10 minutes or until onions begin to brown, stirring occasionally. Stir in water. Reduce heat to medium; partially cover and cook 20 minutes or until onions are deep golden brown, stirring occasionally. Remove from heat; stir in rosemary and pepper. Let cool slightly.

4. Preheat oven to 375°F. Prick dough all over with fork. Sprinkle fontina cheese over dough; top with caramelized onions. Sprinkle with Parmesan cheese.

5. Bake 18 to 20 minutes or until golden brown. Remove from pan to wire rack. Cut into pieces; serve warm.

Makes 12 servings

Calories 160, **Total Fat** 5g, **Saturated Fat** 2g, **Cholesterol** 5mg, **Sodium** 380mg, **Carbohydrate** 22g, **Dietary Fiber** 3g, **Protein** 6g

GOAT CHEESE CROSTINI WITH SWEET ONION JAM Ⓥ Ⓛⓒ

- 2 medium yellow onions
- 1 tablespoon olive oil
- ¾ cup dry red wine
- ¼ cup water
- 2 tablespoons packed brown sugar
- 1 tablespoon balsamic vinegar
- 1 teaspoon salt
- ¼ teaspoon black pepper
- 2 ounces soft goat cheese
- 2 ounces reduced-fat cream cheese, softened
- 1 teaspoon chopped fresh thyme, plus additional for garnish
- 1 loaf (16 ounces) French bread, cut into 24 slices (about 1 inch thick), lightly toasted

1. Spiral onions with thick ribbon blade.

2. Heat oil in large skillet over medium heat. Add onions; cook and stir 10 minutes. Add wine, water, brown sugar, vinegar, salt and pepper; bring to a simmer. Reduce heat to low; cook, uncovered, 15 to 20 minutes or until all liquid is absorbed. (If mixture appears dry, stir in a few tablespoons of additional water.) Cool 30 minutes or cover and refrigerate until ready to use.

3. Meanwhile, stir goat cheese, cream cheese and 1 teaspoon thyme in small bowl until well blended.

4. Spread ½ teaspoon goat cheese mixture on each slice of bread. Top with 1 teaspoon onion jam. Garnish with additional thyme.

Makes 24 crostini

Calories 86, **Total Fat** 2g, **Saturated Fat** <1g, **Cholesterol** 2mg, **Sodium** 215mg, **Carbohydrate** 13g, **Dietary Fiber** <1g, **Protein** 3g

ONION FRITTERS WITH SPIRALED CUCUMBER SAUCE : GF V LC

Onion fritters (bhaji) are a popular Indian snack, appetizer and street food. If you like yours spicy, add ground red pepper or red pepper flakes to the batter; try ⅛ teaspoon at first and then add more if you like.

8 ounces seedless cucumber (about 8 inches)

1 container (7 ounces) reduced-fat Greek yogurt

1 clove garlic, minced

2 teaspoons chopped fresh mint

1 teaspoon salt, divided

2 yellow onions (8 ounces each)

½ cup chickpea flour

½ teaspoon baking powder

¼ teaspoon ground cumin

1 tablespoon minced fresh cilantro

¼ cup water

½ cup vegetable oil

1. For sauce, spiral cucumber with thin ribbon blade and coarsely chop. Combine yogurt, garlic, mint and ½ teaspoon salt in medium bowl. Stir in cucumber. Refrigerate until ready to serve.

2. For fritters, spiral onions with thin ribbon blade. Shape the onions into a pile and make two perpendicular cuts through top.

3. Whisk chickpea flour, baking powder, remaining ½ teaspoon salt and cumin in large bowl. Stir in cilantro. Whisk in water in thin steady stream until batter is the consistency of heavy cream. Add additional water by teaspoonfuls if batter is too thick. Stir in onions until coated with batter.

4. Heat oil in large cast iron skillet over medium-high heat. Working in batches, drop level ¼-cupfuls of onion mixture into hot oil. Cook about 2 minutes or until bottoms are well browned. Turn and press lightly with spatula. Cook 2 minutes or until well browned on both sides. Drain on paper towels. Serve hot with cucumber sauce.

Makes 10 fritters and 1¼ cups sauce

Calories 150, **Total Fat** 12g, **Saturated Fat** 2g, **Cholesterol** 0mg, **Sodium** 270mg, **Carbohydrate** 8g, **Dietary Fiber** 2g, **Protein** 3g

CHORIZO AND CARAMELIZED ONION TORTILLA (GF) (DF) (LC)

3 medium yellow onions

2 tablespoons olive oil

8 ounces Spanish chorizo (about 2 links) or andouille sausage, diced

6 eggs
   Salt and black pepper

½ cup chopped fresh parsley

1. Spiral onions with thick ribbon blade or slicing blade; cut into desired lengths.

2. Heat oil in medium skillet over medium heat. Add onions; cover and cook 10 minutes or until onions are translucent. Reduce heat to low; cook, uncovered, 40 minutes or until golden and very tender. Remove onions from skillet; let cool.

3. Cook chorizo in same skillet over medium heat 5 minutes or just until chorizo begins to brown, stirring occasionally. Remove chorizo from skillet; set aside to cool.

4. Preheat oven to 350°F. Spray 9-inch square baking pan with olive oil cooking spray.

5. Whisk eggs in medium bowl; season with salt and pepper. Add onions, chorizo and parsley; stir gently until well blended. Pour egg mixture into prepared pan.

6. Bake 12 to 15 minutes or until center is almost set. *Turn oven to broil.* Broil 1 to 2 minutes or until top just starts to brown. Cool completely in pan on wire rack. Cut into 18 squares (or 36 triangles); serve cold or at room temperature.

Makes 18 servings

Calories 100, **Total Fat** 8g, **Saturated Fat** 3g, **Cholesterol** 75mg, **Sodium** 180mg, **Carbohydrate** 2g, **Dietary Fiber** 0g, **Protein** 5g

Salads

PEA SALAD WITH CUCUMBERS AND RED ONION GF V LC

This classic summer salad is refreshingly new with spiraled cucumber, onion and bell pepper. Cut the vegetables into 3-inch (or shorter) lengths to make the salad easier to serve and eat.

1 small seedless cucumber

½ red onion

1 red bell pepper

¼ cup reduced-fat mayonnaise

¼ cup reduced-fat sour cream or Greek yogurt

1 tablespoon fresh lemon juice

2 teaspoons chopped fresh mint or oregano

½ teaspoon salt

½ teaspoon black pepper

2 cups frozen green peas, thawed

1. Spiral cucumber and onion with thick ribbon blade. Spiral bell pepper with spiral slicing blade. Cut vegetables into desired lengths.

2. Combine mayonnaise, sour cream, lemon juice, mint, salt and black pepper in large bowl. Stir in peas, cucumber, onion and bell pepper.

Makes 6 to 8 servings

....

Calories 80, **Total Fat** 3g, **Saturated Fat** 1g, **Cholesterol** 5mg, **Sodium** 340mg, **Carbohydrate** 11g, **Dietary Fiber** 3g, **Protein** 4g

....

ZESTY ZUCCHINI CHICKPEA SALAD

This colorful and delicious Mediterranean-inspired salad makes the perfect accompaniment to grilled meats and kabobs. Or stuff it into pita halves with some leafy greens and fresh tomatoes for a quick lunch. Note that chipotle peppers can be quite spicy so start with a small amount and add more to taste until you reach your desired level of heat.

3 medium zucchini

½ teaspoon salt

5 tablespoons white vinegar

1 clove garlic, minced

¼ teaspoon dried thyme

½ cup olive oil

1 cup canned chickpeas, rinsed and drained

½ cup sliced pitted black olives

3 green onions, minced

1 canned chipotle pepper in adobo sauce, drained, seeded and minced

1 ripe avocado

⅓ cup crumbled reduced-fat feta cheese

1. Spiral zucchini with thick ribbon blade; cut into desired lengths. Place in medium bowl; sprinkle with salt and toss to mix. Spread zucchini on several layers of paper towels. Let stand at room temperature 30 minutes to drain.

2. Combine vinegar, garlic and thyme in large bowl. Gradually whisk in oil until dressing is thoroughly blended. Pat zucchini dry; add to dressing. Add chickpeas, olives and green onions; toss lightly to coat. Cover and refrigerate at least 30 minutes or up to 4 hours, stirring occasionally.

3. Stir in chipotle pepper just before serving. Cut avocado into ½-inch cubes. Add avocado and cheese to salad; toss lightly to mix.

Makes 6 servings

Calories 310, **Total Fat** 27g, **Saturated Fat** 4g, **Cholesterol** 0mg, **Sodium** 640mg, **Carbohydrate** 16g, **Dietary Fiber** 6g, **Protein** 6g

GERMAN FRUIT SALAD   GF V LS

This tangy, creamy fruit salad is similar to ambrosia but without the sugary sweetness of marshmallows and coconut.

2 jars (16 ounces each) maraschino cherries, drained

1 large orange, peeled and cut into 1-inch pieces

1 can (20 ounces) pineapple chunks, drained

1 container (16 ounces) reduced-fat sour cream

1 tablespoon reduced-fat mayonnaise

Chopped walnuts (optional)

2 large red apples

2 bananas, cut into bite-size pieces

1. Combine cherries, oranges and pineapple in large bowl.

2. Combine sour cream and mayonnaise in medium bowl; stir into fruit mixture. Add chopped walnuts, if desired; mix well. Cover and refrigerate 2 hours.

3. Spiral apples with spiral slicing blade. Stand apples on cutting board and cut into quarters. Add apples and bananas to salad just before serving; mix well.

Makes 10 servings

Calories 350, **Total Fat** 6g, **Saturated Fat** 4g, **Cholesterol** 25mg, **Sodium** 40mg, **Carbohydrate** 63g, **Dietary Fiber** 3g, **Protein** 3g

BEET AND BLUE CHEESE SALAD

This salad features raw beets, which are quite crunchy and can be difficult to eat in long spirals. If you'd prefer cooked beets, heat 1 teaspoon oil in a medium nonstick skillet over medium heat. Add the beets and cook until they are tender, stirring occasionally. Cut the spiraled vegetables into 2-inch pieces to match the length of the baby spinach leaves.

1 small beet, peeled

½ red onion

2 large carrots

1 package (6 ounces) baby spinach

¼ cup balsamic vinegar

2 tablespoons canola oil

2 tablespoons pure maple syrup

¼ teaspoon salt

⅛ teaspoon red pepper flakes

¼ cup crumbled blue cheese

1. Spiral beet, onion and carrots with thin ribbon blade; cut into desired lengths.

2. Divide spinach among four salad plates. Top evenly with beets, onion and carrots.

3. Whisk vinegar, oil, maple syrup, salt and red pepper flakes in small bowl until smooth and well blended. Drizzle dressing over salad. Sprinkle evenly with cheese.

Makes 4 servings

Calories 150, **Total Fat** 9g, **Saturated Fat** 2g, **Cholesterol** 5mg, **Sodium** 310mg, **Carbohydrate** 16g, **Dietary Fiber** 2g, **Protein** 3g

COLD PEANUT NOODLE AND EDAMAME SALAD DF V V+ HF

This version of classic spicy sesame noodles adds peanut butter and chopped peanuts for a sweet-salty crunch. For less spicy noodles, reduce the sriracha to 1 teaspoon or to taste.

8 ounces uncooked whole wheat spaghetti

8 ounces seedless cucumber (about 8 inches)

2 large carrots

3 tablespoons reduced-sodium soy sauce

2 tablespoons toasted sesame oil

2 tablespoons unseasoned rice vinegar

1 tablespoon sugar

1 tablespoon finely grated fresh ginger

1 tablespoon creamy peanut butter

1 tablespoon sriracha or hot chili sauce

2 teaspoons minced garlic

½ cup thawed frozen shelled edamame

¼ cup sliced green onions

¼ cup chopped peanuts

1. Cook noodles according to package directions. Rinse under cold water; drain. Cut noodles into 3-inch lengths. Place in large bowl; set aside.

2. Spiral cucumber and carrots with thin ribbon blade. Cut into 3-inch lengths.

3. Whisk soy sauce, sesame oil, vinegar, sugar, ginger, peanut butter, sriracha and garlic in small bowl until smooth and well blended. Add to noodles; toss to coat. Stir in edamame, cucumber and carrots. Cover and refrigerate at least 30 minutes to allow flavors to blend.

4. Sprinkle with green onions and peanuts just before serving.

Makes 4 servings

Calories 530, **Total Fat** 26g, **Saturated Fat** 4g, **Cholesterol** 0mg, **Sodium** 780mg, **Carbohydrate** 61g, **Dietary Fiber** 12g, **Protein** 20g

KOHLRABI AND CARROT SLAW

Kohlrabi ("turnip cabbage") is a member of Brassica oleracea along with broccoli, cauliflower, cabbage and kale. Its flavor is similar to broccoli but a bit sweeter. The skin is pretty tough so make sure you use a sturdy peeler.

2 pounds kohlrabi bulbs, peeled

1 small red bell pepper

2 medium carrots, shredded

8 cherry tomatoes, cut into halves

2 green onions, thinly sliced

¼ cup fat-free mayonnaise

¼ cup plain fat-free yogurt

2 tablespoons cider vinegar

2 tablespoons finely chopped fresh parsley

1 teaspoon dried dill weed

¼ teaspoon salt

¼ teaspoon ground cumin

⅛ teaspoon black pepper

1. Spiral kohlrabi with thick ribbon blade; cut into desired lengths. Spiral bell pepper with spiral slicing blade; cut into desired lengths.

2. Combine kohlrabi, carrots, bell pepper, tomatoes and green onions in medium bowl.

3. Combine mayonnaise, yogurt, vinegar, parsley, dill, salt, cumin and black pepper in small bowl until smooth. Add to vegetables; toss to coat. Cover and refrigerate until ready to serve.

Makes 8 servings

Calories 38, **Total Fat** 1g, **Saturated Fat** 0g, **Cholesterol** 1mg, **Sodium** 154mg, **Carbohydrate** 9g, **Dietary Fiber** 2g, **Protein** 2g

ZUCCHINI RIBBON SALAD

2 medium zucchini

2 tablespoons chopped sun-dried tomatoes (not packed in oil)

2 teaspoons olive oil

1 teaspoon fresh lemon juice

1 teaspoon white vinegar

⅛ teaspoon salt

2 tablespoons shredded Parmesan cheese

1 tablespoon pine nuts, toasted*

*To toast pine nuts, spread in single layer in heavy skillet. Cook over medium heat 1 to 2 minutes or until nuts are lightly browned, stirring frequently.

1. Spiral zucchini with thick ribbon blade. Combine zucchini and sun-dried tomatoes in medium bowl.

2. Whisk oil, lemon juice, vinegar and salt in small bowl until well blended. Drizzle over zucchini and tomatoes; toss gently to coat.

3. Top with cheese and pine nuts just before serving.

Makes 4 servings

Calories 67, **Total Fat** 5g, **Saturated Fat** 1g, **Cholesterol** 2mg, **Sodium** 127mg, **Carbohydrate** 5g, **Dietary Fiber** 2g, **Protein** 3g

APPLE-WALNUT SALAD WITH BLUE CHEESE VINAIGRETTE (GF) (V)

- ¼ cup chopped walnuts
- 1 tablespoon white wine vinegar
- 2 teaspoons olive oil
- 2 teaspoons honey
- ¼ teaspoon salt
- ⅛ teaspoon black pepper
- 2 tablespoons crumbled blue cheese
- 1 red apple
- 1 Granny Smith apple
- 1 large head Bibb lettuce, separated into leaves

1. Cook and stir walnuts in small skillet over medium heat 5 minutes or until fragrant and lightly toasted. Transfer to plate to cool.

2. Whisk vinegar, oil, honey, salt and pepper in small bowl until well blended. Stir in cheese.

3. Spiral apples with spiral slicing blade. Stand apples on cutting board and cut in half to make slices.

4. Divide lettuce and apples evenly among four plates. Drizzle dressing evenly over each salad; top with walnuts.

Makes 4 servings

Calories 147, **Total Fat** 8g, **Saturated Fat** 2g, **Cholesterol** 3mg, **Sodium** 207mg, **Carbohydrate** 18g, **Dietary Fiber** 3g, **Protein** 3g

CORN, AVOCADO AND RED ONION SALAD (GF) (DF) (V) (V+) (HF)

This simple salad makes the most of crisp sweet corn and creamy avocados. For maximum crunch and flavor, simply blanch the corn in boiling water or toast it in a medium saucepan in a drizzle of olive oil until fragrant and light golden brown.

½ red onion

1 small green bell pepper

1 cup cooked fresh or thawed frozen corn

1 avocado, diced

1 tablespoon white wine vinegar

¼ teaspoon salt

⅛ teaspoon black pepper

Pinch ground cumin

3 tablespoons olive oil

4 cups mixed salad greens or chopped romaine lettuce

1. Spiral onion with thin ribbon blade. Spiral bell pepper with spiral slicing blade. Cut vegetables into desired lengths. Place in large bowl; fold in corn and avocado.

2. Combine vinegar, salt, pepper and cumin in small bowl; whisk until salt is dissolved. Whisk in oil. Pour over vegetables; mix well. Serve with greens.

Makes 4 servings

Calories 230, **Total Fat** 18g, **Saturated Fat** 3g, **Cholesterol** 0mg, **Sodium** 170mg, **Carbohydrate** 17g, **Dietary Fiber** 6g, **Protein** 3g

FARMERS' MARKET POTATO SALAD

Pickled red onions are a tasty and versatile condiment (and the spiralizer makes preparing them a snap); try them on sandwiches, burgers, grilled meats and in other salads. The following recipe makes just enough to use in this potato salad, but the recipe easily doubles.

Pickled Red Onions (recipe follows)

2 pounds red potatoes

1 cup green beans, cut into 1-inch pieces

2 tablespoons plain nonfat Greek yogurt

2 tablespoons white wine vinegar

2 tablespoons olive oil

1 tablespoon spicy mustard

1 teaspoon salt

1. Prepare Pickled Red Onions. Spiral potatoes with spiral slicing blade. Stand potatoes on cutting board and cut in half to make slices.

2. Bring large saucepan of water to a boil. Add potatoes; cook 4 minutes. Add green beans; cook 2 minutes or until vegetables are fork-tender. Drain and transfer to large bowl. Stir in onions.

3. Whisk yogurt, vinegar, oil, mustard and salt in large bowl until well blended. Pour over vegetables; stir gently to coat. Cover and refrigerate at least 1 hour for flavors to blend.

Makes 6 servings

Pickled Red Onions

1 small red onion

¼ cup white wine vinegar

2 tablespoons water

1 teaspoon sugar

1 teaspoon salt

1. Spiral red onion with thin ribbon blade; cut into desired lengths.

2. Combine all ingredients in large glass jar. Seal jar; shake well. Refrigerate at least 1 hour or up to 1 week. Recipe can be doubled.

Makes about ½ cup

Calories 107, **Total Fat** 5g, **Saturated Fat** 1g, **Cholesterol** 0mg, **Sodium** 628mg, **Carbohydrate** 13g, **Dietary Fiber** 2g, **Protein** 2g

Soups

SAUSAGE, SQUASH AND KALE STEW

Butternut squash, a stubborn vegetable to peel, can likewise resist your efforts to spiralize it. For best results, try spiralizing smaller pieces (about 2 inches long) and switching the side getting spiralized if the grip on the spiralizer begins to slip or drag through the squash.

1 butternut squash, peeled

1 tablespoon vegetable oil

12 ounces hot or mild lean Italian turkey sausage

1 can (about 14 ounces) diced no-salt-added tomatoes

½ cup water

6 cups coarsely chopped stemmed fresh kale or Swiss chard (about 4 ounces)

¼ teaspoon black pepper

¼ cup grated Parmesan or Romano cheese

1. Spiral squash with thick ribbon blade; cut into desired lengths.

2. Heat oil in large saucepan over medium heat. Remove sausage from casings; crumble into saucepan. Cook sausage until browned, stirring to break up meat.

3. Stir in tomatoes with juice and ½ cup water. Top with kale. Reduce heat to medium-low; cover and cook 8 minutes. Stir in squash and pepper; cover and cook 5 minutes or until squash is tender. Ladle into bowls; top with cheese.

Makes 4 servings

Calories 300, **Total Fat** 15g, **Saturated Fat** 5g, **Cholesterol** 70mg, **Sodium** 710mg, **Carbohydrate** 24g, **Dietary Fiber** 5g, **Protein** 22g

TOMATO ONION SOUP · GF V LC

Who doesn't love the classic pairing of tomato soup and grilled cheese? This recipe combines the two with a zesty tomato soup topped with crunchy croutons and melty cheese.

2 large onions

2 tablespoons butter

1 clove garlic, minced

1¾ cups tomato juice

3 cups reduced-sodium vegetable broth

⅔ cup picante sauce

1 cup croutons

1 cup (4 ounces) shredded Monterey Jack cheese

1. Spiral onions with thick ribbon blade; cut into desired lengths.

2. Melt butter in medium saucepan over medium-low heat. Add onions and garlic; cook 20 minutes or until onions are tender and golden brown, stirring occasionally.

3. Stir in tomato juice, broth and picante sauce. Bring to a boil over medium-high heat. Reduce heat to low; simmer 20 minutes.

4. Ladle soup into bowls and sprinkle with croutons and cheese.

Makes 6 servings

Calories 180, **Total Fat** 10g, **Saturated Fat** 6g, **Cholesterol** 25mg, **Sodium** 540mg, **Carbohydrate** 15g, **Dietary Fiber** 2g, **Protein** 6g

LENTIL VEGETABLE STEW

At first glance this spiraly stew might not seem very interesting (lentils, cauliflower, yellow squash—boring, right?), but it will surprise you with its fragrant, tangy tomato broth and hearty, satisfying combination of vegetables.

1 large onion

3 tablespoons vegetable oil

1 can (28 ounces) crushed tomatoes

2 cups water

1 tablespoon curry powder

1½ teaspoons ground cumin

1½ teaspoons ground coriander

1 teaspoon ground ginger

1½ teaspoons salt

1 tablespoon cider vinegar

1¼ cups dried brown or green lentils, rinsed and sorted

1 red bell pepper

1 yellow squash

2 cups cauliflower florets

1. Spiral onion with spiral slicing blade; cut into 1-inch pieces.

2. Heat oil in large saucepan over medium heat. Add onion; cook and stir 5 minutes or until softened. Stir in tomatoes, water, curry powder, cumin, coriander, ginger, salt and vinegar. Stir in lentils; bring to a boil. Reduce heat to medium-low; simmer 35 to 40 minutes or until lentils begin to soften.

3. Spiral bell pepper and yellow squash with spiral slicing blade. Stand squash vertically and cut in half to make slices; cut bell pepper into desired lengths.

4. Add cauliflower, bell pepper and squash to stew; cook 30 to 40 minutes or until vegetables and lentils are tender.

Makes 8 servings

Calories 210, **Total Fat** 6g, **Saturated Fat** <1g, **Cholesterol** 0mg, **Sodium** 640mg, **Carbohydrate** 32g, **Dietary Fiber** 9g, **Protein** 9g

CURRIED VEGETABLE-RICE SOUP

With an array of fresh vegetables, brown rice and creamy coconut milk, this soup is a meal on its own. For lunch, pack portions in jars or food storage containers; reheat it in the microwave and refresh with a bit more lime juice.

1 red bell pepper

1 small onion

1 small zucchini

2 teaspoons vegetable oil

1 cup broccoli or cauliflower florets

1 can (about 14 ounces) reduced-sodium vegetable broth

¾ cup uncooked instant brown rice

2 teaspoons curry powder

½ teaspoon salt

½ teaspoon hot pepper sauce

1 can (14 ounces) light unsweetened coconut milk

1 tablespoon lime juice

1. Spiral bell pepper, onion and zucchini with spiral slicing blade. Stand zucchini on end and cut in half to make slices. Cut bell pepper and onion into desired lengths.

2. Heat oil in large saucepan over medium-high heat. Add bell pepper, onion, zucchini and broccoli; cook and stir 5 minutes or until vegetables are softened. Add broth; bring to a boil over high heat.

3. Stir in rice, curry powder, salt and hot pepper sauce. Reduce heat to medium-low; cover and simmer 8 minutes or until rice is tender, stirring once.

4. Stir in coconut milk; cook 3 minutes or until heated through. Remove from heat; stir in lime juice. Serve immediately.

Makes 4 servings

Calories 180, **Total Fat** 8g, **Saturated Fat** 4g, **Cholesterol** 0mg, **Sodium** 420mg, **Carbohydrate** 25g, **Dietary Fiber** 4g, **Protein** 3g

CLASSIC FRENCH ONION SOUP

3 large yellow onions (about 2 pounds)

2 tablespoons butter

1 cup dry white wine

3 cans (about 14 ounces each) reduced-sodium beef or chicken broth

½ teaspoon salt (optional)

¼ teaspoon white pepper

1 bouquet garni*

4 slices (1-inch thick) French bread

4 ounces finely shredded Gruyère cheese

*To prepare bouquet garni, tie together 3 fresh parsley sprigs, 2 fresh thyme sprigs and ½ bay leaf with cotton string or enclose herbs in square of cheesecloth secured with string.

1. Spiral onions with thick ribbon blade; cut into desired lengths.

2. Heat butter in Dutch oven over medium-high heat. Add onions; cook and stir 15 minutes or until lightly browned. Reduce heat to medium; cook 30 to 45 minutes until onions are golden brown, stirring occasionally.

3. Add wine to Dutch oven; cook over high heat 3 to 5 minutes or until liquid is reduced by half, stirring to scrape up browned bits. Add broth, salt, if desired, pepper and bouquet garni; bring to a boil. Reduce heat to low; simmer 20 minutes. Remove bouquet garni.

4. Preheat broiler. Broil bread about 3 minutes per side or until lightly toasted.

5. Ladle soup into four heatproof bowls; top with toast and cheese. Broil 4 inches from heat 2 to 3 minutes or until cheese is bubbly and browned. Serve immediately.

Makes 4 servings

Calories 440, **Total Fat** 15g, **Saturated Fat** 9g, **Cholesterol** 55mg, **Sodium** 1130mg, **Carbohydrate** 47g, **Dietary Fiber** 5g, **Protein** 18g

BARLEY STEW WITH CORNMEAL-CHEESE DUMPLINGS Ⓥ ⒽⒻ

1 medium zucchini

4 large carrots

1 parsnip, peeled

2 cans (11½ ounces each) reduced-sodium spicy vegetable juice cocktail

1 can (about 15 ounces) butter beans, drained

1 can (about 14 ounces) no-salt-added stewed tomatoes, undrained

1 cup water

½ cup quick pearl barley

1 bay leaf

2 tablespoons chopped fresh thyme

1½ tablespoons chopped fresh rosemary leaves

1 cup all-purpose flour

⅓ cup cornmeal

2 teaspoons baking powder

½ cup reduced-fat (2%) milk

2 tablespoons canola oil

1 cup (4 ounces) shredded reduced-fat Cheddar cheese

1. Spiral zucchini, carrots and parsnip with thick ribbon blade.

2. Combine vegetable juice, beans, tomatoes with juice, water, barley, bay leaf, thyme and rosemary in large saucepan. Bring to a boil over high heat. Reduce heat to medium-low. Cover; simmer 20 to 25 minutes or until tender, stirring occasionally. Remove and discard bay leaf.

3. Combine flour, cornmeal and baking powder in small bowl. Combine milk and oil in separate small bowl; stir into flour mixture. Stir in cheese.

4. Drop dough by spoonfuls into eight mounds onto boiling stew. Cover and simmer 10 to 12 minutes or until toothpick inserted near center of dumplings comes out clean.

Makes 8 servings

Calories 330, **Total Fat** 8g, **Saturated Fat** 3g, **Cholesterol** 10mg, **Sodium** 480mg, **Carbohydrate** 54g, **Dietary Fiber** 10g, **Protein** 12g

Main Dishes

GINGER PORK STIR-FRY ON SOBA

Soba noodles are Japanese buckwheat noodles (naturally gluten-free) that have a dark brown color and a slightly chewy texture. Look for them in the Asian section of well-stocked supermarkets.

12 ounces pork tenderloin, trimmed

2 tablespoons reduced-sodium tamari, divided

2 teaspoons grated fresh ginger

1 clove garlic, minced

1 small seedless cucumber

1 small red onion

2 teaspoons coconut or vegetable oil

2 cups fresh sugar snap peas

1 teaspoon dark sesame oil

¼ teaspoon hot chili oil or red pepper flakes

1 tablespoon minced fresh chives

2 teaspoons minced fresh cilantro

2 ounces soba noodles, cooked according to package directions

1. Cut pork into thin strips, about 1 inch long.* Place in large bowl. Add 1 tablespoon tamari, ginger and garlic; stir well. Cover and refrigerate 1 to 2 hours, stirring occasionally.

2. Spiral cucumber with thin ribbon blade; cut into desired lengths. Set aside. Spiral onion with thin ribbon blade; cut into desired lengths.

3. Heat coconut oil in large nonstick skillet over medium-high heat. Add peas and onion; cook and stir 5 to 6 minutes or until peas are crisp-tender. Transfer to bowl.

4. Add pork and marinade to same skillet; cook and stir 3 to 5 minutes or until pork is cooked through. Add remaining 1 tablespoon tamari, sesame oil and chili oil. Stir in peas and onion, chives and cilantro; cook and stir until heated through.

5. Toss cucumber with soba noodles in medium bowl; arrange on four serving plates. Top with pork mixture.

Makes 4 servings

*Freeze pork 30 minutes to make slicing easier.

Calories 220, **Total Fat** 5g, **Saturated Fat** 3g, **Cholesterol** 55mg, **Sodium** 370mg, **Carbohydrate** 20g, **Dietary Fiber** 2g, **Protein** 23g

VEGETABLE ENCHILADAS (GF) (V) (HF)

Poblano peppers spiralize surprisingly well. Use the spiral slicing blade, rather than one of the ribbon blades. Trim the stem off the pepper but do not remove the whole stem end; this helps stabilize the pepper and gives the spiralizer something to grip while spiraling.

1 large zucchini

1 large red onion

2 large poblano peppers or green bell peppers

1 tablespoon vegetable oil

1 cup sliced mushrooms

1 teaspoon ground cumin

1 pound fresh tomatillos (about 8 large), peeled

½ to 1 jalapeño pepper, minced

1 clove garlic

½ teaspoon salt

1 cup loosely packed fresh cilantro

12 corn tortillas, warmed

2 cups (8 ounces) shredded Mexican cheese blend, divided

1. Preheat oven to 400°F.

2. Spiral zucchini and red onion with thick ribbon blade. Spiral poblano peppers with spiral slicing blade. Cut vegetables into desired lengths.

3. Heat oil in large skillet over medium heat. Add poblano peppers, zucchini, onion, mushrooms and cumin; cook and stir 8 to 10 minutes or until crisp-tender.

4. Meanwhile, place tomatillos in large microwavable bowl. Cover with vented plastic wrap. Microwave on HIGH 6 to 7 minutes or until very tender.

5. Combine tomatillos with juice, jalapeño pepper, garlic and salt in food processor or blender; process until smooth. Add cilantro; pulse until combined and cilantro is coarsely chopped.

6. Divide vegetables evenly among tortillas. Spoon heaping tablespoon of cheese in center of each tortilla; roll up to enclose filling. Place in 13×9-inch baking dish; top with sauce. Sprinkle with remaining 1 cup cheese.

7. Bake, covered, 18 to 20 minutes or until cheese is melted and enchiladas are heated through.

Makes 6 servings

Calories 330, **Total Fat** 16g, **Saturated Fat** 7g, **Cholesterol** 35mg, **Sodium** 340mg, **Carbohydrate** 35g, **Dietary Fiber** 6g, **Protein** 14g

ROASTED TURKEY WITH CILANTRO-LIME BUTTERNUT SQUASH GF DF LC

1½ tablespoons chili powder

2 teaspoons dried oregano

1½ teaspoons ground cumin

½ teaspoon red pepper flakes

1½ teaspoons salt, divided

½ teaspoon black pepper

1 bone-in turkey breast with skin (5 pounds)

1 butternut squash, peeled and seeded

2 red bell peppers

2½ cups water

½ teaspoon ground turmeric

1 cup chopped green onions

½ cup chopped fresh cilantro

3 tablespoons olive oil

2 tablespoons fresh lime juice

1 tablespoon grated lime peel

1. Preheat oven to 325°F. Spray roasting pan and rack with nonstick cooking spray. Combine chili powder, oregano, cumin, red pepper flakes, ½ teaspoon salt and black pepper in small bowl.

2. Separate turkey skin from meat by sliding fingers under skin. Spread chili mixture evenly over meat; cover with skin. (If skin tears, use toothpick to hold skin together.) Place turkey breast on prepared rack in roasting pan, skin side up.

3. Roast 1 hour and 30 minutes or until meat thermometer reaches 165°F. Remove from oven. Cover loosely with foil; let stand 10 to 15 minutes. Remove and discard skin, if desired.

4. Spiral squash with thick ribbon blade; place in food processor. Pulse until small pieces form. Spiral bell peppers with spiral slicing blade; cut into desired lengths.

5. Combine bell peppers, water, squash and turmeric in large saucepan. Bring to a boil. Reduce heat; cover and simmer 10 minutes or until liquid evaporates. Remove from heat; stir in green onions, cilantro, oil, lime juice, lime peel and remaining ¾ teaspoon salt. Serve with turkey.

Makes 12 servings

Calories 230, **Total Fat** 6g, **Saturated Fat** 1g, **Cholesterol** 95mg, **Sodium** 400mg, **Carbohydrate** 7g, **Dietary Fiber** 2g, **Protein** 36g

SESAME GINGER TOFU BÁHN MÌ

4 ounces peeled daikon radish *or* 5 red radishes

1 large carrot

1 tablespoon granulated sugar

¾ cup unseasoned rice vinegar

½ teaspoon salt

1 clove garlic

1 piece (1 inch) peeled fresh ginger

¼ cup reduced-sodium soy sauce

1 tablespoon packed brown sugar

1 tablespoon dark sesame oil

1 package (14 ounces) extra firm tofu, drained, pressed and halved crosswise

8 ounces seedless cucumber (about 8 inches)

1 tablespoon vegetable oil

1 loaf (16 ounces) soft French bread

¼ cup mayonnaise

Fresh cilantro sprigs

1 jalapeño pepper, sliced into rings

1. Spiral radish and carrot with thin ribbon blade. Stir granulated sugar into vinegar in 2-cup measuring cup until dissolved; stir in salt. Measure 1 cup total of carrots and radish; add to vinegar. Let stand at least 1 hour for flavors to blend.

2. Place garlic and ginger in food processor; process until minced. Add soy sauce, brown sugar and sesame oil; blend until smooth.

3. Place tofu in 8-inch square baking dish; top with marinade. Marinate at room temperature 30 minutes to 1 hour, turning occasionally.

4. Drain tofu, discarding marinade. Heat vegetable oil in cast iron skillet over high heat. Working in batches, cook tofu 3 to 4 minutes per side or until well browned. Let stand until cool enough to handle. Cut into thin slices.

5. Spiral cucumber with thick ribbon blade. Cut bread into individual portions; scoop out some of soft insides. Spread mayonnaise over bottoms of bread; top with tofu, cucumber, pickled radish mixture, cilantro and jalapeños.

Makes 8 servings

Sesame Ginger Pork Báhn Mì: Prepare marinade as directed in step 2; pour into large resealable food storage bad. Add 1 pork tenderloin (about 1 pound); seal bag and turn to coat. Marinate in refrigerator 1 hour. Drain pork; place in greased baking dish. Bake at 400°F for 30 minutes or until pork is 145°F. Let stand until cool enough to handle. Cut into thin slices.

Calories 390, **Total Fat** 10g, **Saturated Fat** 2g, **Cholesterol** 0mg, **Sodium** 1200mg, **Carbohydrate** 62g, **Dietary Fiber** 4g, **Protein** 14g

ROASTED SALMON WITH LENTILS AND SQUASH GF DF HF

Lentils, a good source of protein, iron and soluble fiber, make a hearty addition to this simple dish of salmon, vegetables and pesto.

- ¾ cup dried brown lentils, rinsed and sorted
- 2 cups water
- 1 teaspoon salt, divided
- ½ cup prepared pesto
- 1 teaspoon grated lemon peel
- ¼ cup fresh lemon juice
- 1 pound salmon fillet (1½ inches thick)
- ¼ teaspoon black pepper, divided
- 1 onion
- 1 yellow squash
- 1 red bell pepper
- 1 teaspoon vegetable oil

1. Preheat oven to 400°F. Line shallow baking pan with foil; spray with nonstick cooking spray.

2. Combine lentils, 2 cups water and ½ teaspoon salt in medium saucepan. Bring to a boil. Reduce heat; simmer 15 to 18 minutes or until lentils are just tender. Drain.

3. Meanwhile, combine pesto, lemon peel and lemon juice in small bowl; mix well. Set aside.

4. Sprinkle salmon with remaining ½ teaspoon salt and ⅛ teaspoon black pepper. Place in prepared baking pan. Bake 10 minutes or until fish just begins to flake when tested with fork.

5. Spiral onion and squash with thin ribbon blade. Spiral bell pepper with spiral slicing blade. Cut vegetables into desired lengths.

6. Heat oil in large nonstick skillet over medium heat. Add bell pepper and onion; cook and stir 3 minutes. Add squash; cook about 5 minutes or until crisp-tender, stirring frequently. Stir in lentils, ¼ cup pesto mixture and remaining ⅛ teaspoon black pepper. Divide vegetable mixture evenly among four serving plates.

7. Cut salmon into four pieces; place on vegetable mixture. Spread remaining pesto mixture over salmon.

Makes 4 servings

Calories 395, **Total Fat** 15g, **Saturated Fat** 3g, **Cholesterol** 68mg, **Sodium** 561mg, **Carbohydrate** 30g, **Dietary Fiber** 13g, **Protein** 34g

PORK WITH SWEET POTATOES AND ONIONS (GF) (DF) (LS)

This recipe is easily doubled, although you'll have to cook the vegetables in two batches. Keep the first batch warm in a covered bowl or on an oven-safe plate in a 200°F oven while you're cooking the second batch.

2 medium sweet potatoes, peeled

½ yellow onion

2 teaspoons olive oil, divided

⅛ teaspoon ground allspice

⅛ teaspoon ground cinnamon

⅛ teaspoon onion powder

¼ teaspoon black pepper

2 boneless pork loin cutlets

1. Spiral sweet potatoes and onion with thin ribbon blade; cut into desired lengths.

2. Heat 1 teaspoon oil in large nonstick skillet over medium-high heat. Add onion; cook 2 minutes or until translucent. Add sweet potatoes, allspice and cinnamon; cook 5 to 10 minutes or until sweet potatoes are lightly browned and tender. Transfer to plate.

3. Sprinkle onion powder and pepper over both sides of pork. Heat remaining 1 teaspoon oil in same skillet over medium heat. Add pork; cook 3 minutes per side or until cooked through. Serve with sweet potatoes and onions.

Makes 2 servings

....

Calories 358, **Total Fat** 12g, **Saturated Fat** 4g, **Cholesterol** 52mg, **Sodium** 73mg, **Carbohydrate** 26g, **Dietary Fiber** 4g, **Protein** 18g

....

SHRIMP AND SAUSAGE SKILLET DINNER (GF) (DF) (LC)

To save time, you can substitute jarred roasted red peppers for the freshly roasted pepper and skip all of step 1. Drain the peppers and rinse well to remove any seeds and oil. Chop enough peppers to measure ½ cup.

1 red bell pepper

1 small rutabaga, peeled

1 teaspoon olive oil

1 onion, chopped

1 clove garlic, minced

2 chicken chorizo sausage links (2 ounces each), thinly sliced

½ cup reduced-sodium chicken broth

6 ounces large raw shrimp, peeled, deveined and cut into bite-size pieces

1 cup frozen green peas

¼ teaspoon salt

¼ teaspoon black pepper

¼ teaspoon smoked paprika

1. Place bell pepper on rack in broiler pan 3 to 5 inches from heat source or hold over open gas flame on long-handled metal fork. Turn bell pepper often until blistered and charred on all sides. Transfer to food storage bag; seal bag and let stand 15 to 20 minutes to loosen skin. Remove loosened skin with paring knife. Cut off top and scrape out seeds. Chop pepper; set aside.

2. Spiral rutabaga with thick ribbon blade. Place in food processor; pulse until small pieces form.

3. Heat oil in large nonstick skillet over medium-high heat. Add onion and garlic; cook and stir 3 minutes. Add sausage; cook and stir 2 minutes or until browned. Pour in broth, stirring to scrape up browned bits.

4. Stir shrimp, bell pepper, peas, rutabaga, salt, black pepper and paprika into skillet. Reduce heat to low; cover and simmer 10 minutes or until rutabaga is tender and mixture is heated through.

Makes 4 servings

Calories 170, **Total Fat** 6g, **Saturated Fat** 2g, **Cholesterol** 85mg, **Sodium** 660mg, **Carbohydrate** 15g, **Dietary Fiber** 4g, **Protein** 15g

SAUSAGE, POTATO AND APPLE BAKE

This colorful casserole with fill your home with the scent of autumn as it bakes. It is perfect as a meal on chilly evenings with toasted French bread, or serve it as a side on Thanksgiving or other festive occasions.

3 tablespoons packed brown sugar

1 tablespoon dried thyme

1 tablespoon dried oregano

¼ cup dry white wine or apple cider

2 tablespoons cider vinegar

2 sweet potatoes (1½ to 2 pounds total), peeled

2 apples, such as Fuji or McIntosh, peeled

1 white onion

1 red bell pepper

1 yellow bell pepper

½ cup golden raisins

1½ pounds smoked sausage, such as kielbasa or Polish sausage, sliced diagonally into ¼-inch pieces

1. Preheat oven to 450°F. Spray 13×9-inch baking dish or 2-quart casserole with nonstick cooking spray.

2. Combine brown sugar, thyme and oregano in large bowl. Stir in white wine and vinegar until brown sugar is dissolved.

3. Spiral sweet potatoes, apples and onion with thick ribbon blade. Spiral bell peppers with spiral slicing blade. Cut vegetables into desired lengths. Add vegetables and raisins to brown sugar mixture; toss to coat.

4. Transfer vegetables to prepared baking dish using tongs or slotted spoon. Mix in sausage; drizzle with remaining brown sugar mixture. Bake 20 minutes or until vegetables are tender.

Makes 8 servings

....

Calories 450, **Total Fat** 25g, **Saturated Fat** 9g, **Cholesterol** 55mg, **Sodium** 800mg, **Carbohydrate** 45g, **Dietary Fiber** 6g, **Protein** 11g

....

SPIRALED BEET RISOTTO

Tender earthy beets combine with creamy rice and tangy cheese in this striking risotto. For a vibrant red risotto, stir the beets into the risotto after one third of broth has been added instead of sautéing them separately in step 2.

1 medium leek, white and light green part

2 medium beets, peeled

4 cups reduced-sodium vegetable broth

2 tablespoons unsalted butter

1 cup uncooked arborio rice

½ cup white wine

1 teaspoon dried Italian seasoning

1 teaspoon salt (optional)

½ cup crumbled goat cheese or shredded Parmesan cheese, plus additional for garnish

1. Spiral leek with spiral slicing blade; coarsely chop to shorten long pieces. Spiral beets with thin ribbon blade; cut into desired lengths.

2. Bring broth to a simmer in medium saucepan over medium heat. Spray large nonstick skillet with nonstick cooking spray; heat over medium-high heat. Add beets; cook and stir 8 to 10 minutes or until tender. Set aside.

3. Melt butter in Dutch oven or large saucepan over medium-high heat. Add leek; cook and stir about 2 minutes or until softened. Add rice; cook about 3 minutes or until rice is translucent around edges, stirring frequently. Add wine; cook and stir until wine is absorbed.

4. Add broth, ½ cup at a time, stirring frequently until broth is absorbed before adding next ½ cup. Continue adding broth and stirring until rice and beets are tender and mixture is creamy, about 20 to 25 minutes total (you may not need all of broth). Remove from heat; fold in beets.

5. Stir in Italian seasoning and salt, if desired; fold in ½ cup cheese. Garnish with additional cheese.

Makes 4 servings

Calories 330, **Total Fat** 10g, **Saturated Fat** 6g, **Cholesterol** 35mg, **Sodium** 240mg, **Carbohydrate** 49g, **Dietary Fiber** 5g, **Protein** 8g

BAKED VEGETABLE PENNE · Ⓥ ⒣Ⓕ

This casserole is sure to please even the pickiest little eaters. Silly vegetable squiggles mixed with chewy whole wheat pasta, all covered with creamy ricotta and classic tomato sauce, is guaranteed to get everyone to eat their veggies.

6 ounces (about 2 cups) uncooked whole wheat penne or ziti pasta

1 large zucchini

1 yellow squash

1 red onion

1 red bell pepper

1 tablespoon vegetable or canola oil

2 cups sliced mushrooms

1 teaspoon salt

1 teaspoon dried Italian seasoning

½ cup part-skim ricotta cheese

2 cups pasta sauce, divided

½ cup (2 ounces) shredded part-skim mozzarella cheese

1. Preheat oven to 400°F. Spray 11×7-inch baking dish with nonstick cooking spray. Cook pasta according to package directions. Drain and return to saucepan; keep warm.

2. Spiral zucchini, yellow squash and red onion with thin ribbon blade. Spiral bell pepper with spiral slicing blade. Cut vegetables into desired lengths.

3. Heat oil in large nonstick skillet over medium-high heat. Add mushrooms; cook and stir 2 to 3 minutes or until browned. Stir in zucchini, squash, onion, bell pepper, salt and Italian seasoning. Remove from heat.

4. Add ricotta cheese and 1½ cups pasta sauce to pasta. Spread half of mixture into prepared baking dish. Layer with vegetable mixture, remaining pasta mixture, pasta sauce and mozzarella cheese.

5. Bake 20 minutes or until cheese is melted and lightly browned. Let stand 15 minutes before serving.

Makes 6 servings

Calories 260, **Total Fat** 8g, **Saturated Fat** 2.5g, **Cholesterol** 15mg, **Sodium** 740mg, **Carbohydrate** 37g, **Dietary Fiber** 8g, **Protein** 12g

SIRLOIN WITH SWEET CARAMELIZED ONIONS (GF) (DF) (LC) (LS)

1 medium onion

1 boneless beef top sirloin steak (about 1 pound)

¼ cup water

2 tablespoons Worcestershire sauce

1 tablespoon sugar

1. Spiral onion with spiral slicing blade; cut into desired lengths.

2. Lightly coat 12-inch skillet with nonstick cooking spray; heat over high heat. Add onion; cook and stir 4 minutes or until browned. Transfer to bowl; set aside. Wipe out skillet with paper towel.

3. Coat same skillet with cooking spray; heat over high heat. Add beef; cook 5 to 7 minutes per side for medium-rare to medium, turning once. Remove from heat and transfer steak to cutting board; let stand 3 minutes before slicing.

4. Meanwhile, return skillet to high heat; add onion, water, Worcestershire sauce and sugar. Cook 30 to 45 seconds or until most liquid has evaporated.

5. Thinly slice beef on the diagonal; serve with onions.

Makes 4 servings

Calories 159, **Total Fat** 5g, **Saturated Fat** 2g, **Cholesterol** 60mg, **Sodium** 118mg, **Carbohydrate** 7g, **Dietary Fiber** 1g, **Protein** 21g

CHICKEN AND SHRIMP JAMBALAYA

If you're looking to reduce your carb intake, or just eat more veggies, try replacing rice with chopped spiraled vegetables. This recipe uses rutabaga but butternut squash, golden beets and sweet potatoes all work well with this technique.

1 medium rutabaga, peeled

1 large onion

1 *each* red, yellow and green bell pepper

2½ to 3 cups fat-free reduced-sodium chicken broth, divided

¾ teaspoon salt (optional)

⅛ teaspoon black pepper

⅛ teaspoon ground red pepper

8 ounces boneless skinless chicken breasts, cut into ½-inch pieces

1 tablespoon vegetable oil

2 cloves garlic, minced

1 large ripe tomato, chopped

6 ounces raw medium shrimp, peeled and deveined

2 tablespoons chopped fresh parsley

1. Spiral rutabaga with thick ribbon blade. Place in food processor; pulse until chopped into rice-size pieces. Spiral onion with thin ribbon blade; cut vegetables into desired lengths. Spiral bell peppers with spiral slicing blade.

2. Bring 2 cups broth to a boil in medium saucepan. Add rutabaga; cook 5 to 7 minutes or until tender. Drain and return to saucepan; keep warm.

3. Meanwhile, combine salt, if desired, black pepper and ground red pepper in small bowl; sprinkle half of mixture over chicken. Heat oil in large nonstick skillet over medium heat. Add chicken; cook without stirring 2 minutes or until golden. Turn chicken; cook 2 minutes. Transfer chicken to plate; set aside.

4. Add onion and bell peppers to same skillet; cook and stir 2 to 3 minutes or until onion is translucent. Add garlic; cook 1 minute. Stir in chicken, tomato, shrimp, remaining pepper mixture and ½ cup chicken broth; bring to a boil. Reduce heat; simmer 5 minutes or until shrimp are opaque.

5. Stir in parsley and rutabaga. Add additional chicken broth if mixture appears dry. Cook 3 minutes longer or until liquid is absorbed and jambalaya is hot.

Makes 4 servings

Calories 220, **Total Fat** 6g, **Saturated Fat** 1g, **Cholesterol** 95mg, **Sodium** 550mg, **Carbohydrate** 21g, **Dietary Fiber** 5g, **Protein** 21g

THAI VEGGIE CURRY   HF

Ribbons of tender sweet potato make a perfect base for this creamy curry. Use more curry paste if you like a spicier sauce but always taste before adding more because spice levels vary among brands. Feel free to substitute any vegetables for the cauliflower and snow peas; try frozen peas, baby corn, carrots or zucchini.

1 onion

2 red or yellow bell peppers

2 sweet potatoes, peeled

4 tablespoons coconut or vegetable oil, divided

1 tablespoon red curry paste (or to taste)

1 can (about 13 ounces) unsweetened light coconut milk

1½ cups cauliflower and/or broccoli florets

1 cup snow peas

1 package (about 14 ounces) tofu, pressed* and cubed

Salt and black pepper

¼ cup slivered fresh basil

Cut tofu in half horizontally and place it between layers of paper towels. Place a weighted cutting board on top; let stand 15 to 30 minutes.

1. Spiral onion and bell peppers with spiral slicing blade. Spiral sweet potatoes with thick ribbon blade. Cut vegetables into desired lengths.

2. Heat 2 tablespoons oil in large skillet over medium heat. Add sweet potatoes; cook and stir 10 to 15 minutes or until sweet potatoes are tender. Transfer to bowl; keep warm.

3. Heat remaining 2 tablespoons oil in same skillet over medium heat. Add onion; cook and stir 2 minutes or until softened. Add curry paste; cook and stir to coat onion. Add coconut milk; bring to a boil, stirring to dissolve curry paste.

4. Add bell peppers and cauliflower; simmer over medium heat 4 to 5 minutes or until crisp-tender. Stir in snow peas; simmer 2 minutes. Gently stir in tofu; cook until heated through. Season with salt and black pepper, if desired. Sprinkle with basil; serve over sweet potato noodles.

Makes 4 servings

Calories 350, **Total Fat** 22g, **Saturated Fat** 14g, **Cholesterol** 0mg, **Sodium** 570mg, **Carbohydrate** 25g, **Dietary Fiber** 6g, **Protein** 16g

SPIRALED SWEET POTATO AND BLACK BEAN TACOS GF V HF

Save any leftover vegetables and black beans to make chilaquiles for dinner the next night (or make extras to ensure leftovers). Heat 2 teaspoons oil in a large nonstick skillet; add some corn tortilla strips and fry until crisp. Add leftover vegetables and beans and cook until heated through. Push everything to one side of the skillet and add four lightly beaten eggs; cook until eggs are softly scrambled and then gently mix everything together. Top with salsa, cilantro, avocado and cheese.

¼ cup reduced-fat sour cream

2 tablespoons reduced-fat mayonnaise

Juice of 1 lime

½ teaspoon chipotle chili powder

1 can (about 15 ounces) black beans, undrained

1 teaspoon smoked paprika

1 sweet potato, peeled

1 red onion

1 green bell pepper

4 teaspoons vegetable oil, divided

¼ teaspoon salt

1 avocado, sliced

¼ cup chopped fresh cilantro

¼ cup grated cotija cheese

8 (6-inch) corn tortillas

1. Combine sour cream, mayonnaise, lime juice and chili powder in small bowl; mix well. Refrigerate until ready to use.

2. Combine beans and paprika in small saucepan. Cook over medium-low heat 5 to 7 minutes or until heated through, stirring occasionally. Remove from heat; coarsely mash beans, leaving some whole. Keep warm.

3. Spiral sweet potato with thick ribbon blade. Spiral onion and bell pepper with spiral slicing blade; cut vegetables into desired lengths.

4. Heat 2 teaspoons oil in medium nonstick skillet over medium heat. Add sweet potato; cook and stir 7 to 10 minutes or until tender. Sprinkle with salt.

5. Heat remaining 2 teaspoons oil in large nonstick skillet over high heat. Add onion and bell pepper; cook and stir 5 minutes or until vegetables are browned and softened.

6. Serve beans, sweet potatoes, vegetables, sour cream mixture, avocado, cilantro and cheese on tortillas; fold in half.

Makes 4 servings

Calories 230, **Total Fat** 12g, **Saturated Fat** 3g, **Cholesterol** 10mg, **Sodium** 340mg, **Carbohydrate** 25g, **Dietary Fiber** 6g, **Protein** 6g

HAVARTI AND ONION SANDWICHES

You probably don't think "sandwich" when you think "spiralizer," but this recipe pairs the two perfectly. Coleslaw made with spiraled cabbage works as a sandwich topping, while leftovers can be served as a side.

½ cup Creamy Coleslaw (recipe follows)

½ red onion

1 teaspoon olive oil

4 slices pumpernickel bread

3 ounces havarti cheese, cut into slices

1. Prepare Creamy Coleslaw.

2. Spiral onion with spiral slicing blade. Heat oil in large skillet over medium heat. Add onion; cook and stir 5 minutes or until tender. Layer two slices of bread with onion, cheese and coleslaw; top with remaining bread.

3. Heat same skillet over medium heat. Add sandwiches; press down with spatula. Cook 4 to 5 minutes per side or until cheese is melted and bread is browned.

Makes 2 sandwiches

Creamy Coleslaw

½ cup reduced-fat mayonnaise

½ cup low-fat buttermilk

2 teaspoons sugar

1 teaspoon celery seed

1 teaspoon fresh lime juice

½ teaspoon chili powder

½ *each* small heads of red and green cabbage

1 cup shredded carrots

¼ cup finely chopped red onion

1. Prepare Creamy Coleslaw.

2. Spiral onion with spiral slicing blade. Heat oil in large skillet over medium heat. Add onion; cook and stir 5 minutes or until tender. Layer two slices of bread with onion, cheese and coleslaw; top with remaining bread.

3. Heat same skillet over medium heat. Add sandwiches; press down with spatula. Cook 4 to 5 minutes per side or until cheese is melted and bread is browned.

Makes 2 sandwiches

Calories 450, **Total Fat** 22g, **Saturated Fat** 11g, **Cholesterol** 45mg, **Sodium** 960mg, **Carbohydrate** 46g, **Dietary Fiber** 6g, **Protein** 16g

Noodles & Zoodles

PESTO ZOODLES WITH POTATOES

The combination of pasta, potatoes and pesto is a classic Italian dish from Liguria, the coastal northwestern region of Italy known for its basil and pesto. In this version, zucchini and potatoes, both cut in the same shape, stand in for the pasta.

3 medium red potatoes

1 large zucchini

¾ cup frozen peas

1 cup packed fresh basil leaves

½ cup pine nuts, toasted*

2 cloves garlic

¾ teaspoon salt, divided

¼ teaspoon black pepper

¼ cup plus 1 tablespoon olive oil, divided

¼ cup plus 2 tablespoons grated Parmesan cheese, divided

Place pine nuts in small saucepan. Heat over low heat 2 minutes or until light brown and fragrant, shaking occasionally.

1. Spiral potatoes and zucchini with thin ribbon blade; cut into desired lengths.

2. Bring medium saucepan of water to a boil. Add potatoes; cook 5 to 7 minutes or until tender, adding peas and zucchini during last 2 minutes of cooking. Drain well; return to saucepan.

3. Meanwhile, place basil, pine nuts, garlic, ½ teaspoon salt and pepper in food processor; drizzle with 1 tablespoon oil. Process about 10 seconds or until coarsely chopped. With motor running, drizzle in remaining ¼ cup oil. Process about 30 seconds or until almost smooth.

4. Add pesto, ¼ cup cheese and remaining ¼ teaspoon salt to vegetables, tossing gently until blended. Sprinkle with remaining 2 tablespoons cheese just before serving.

Makes 6 servings

Calories 370, **Total Fat** 26g, **Saturated Fat** 6g, **Cholesterol** 10mg, **Sodium** 470mg, **Carbohydrate** 25g, **Dietary Fiber** 6g, **Protein** 9g

PAD THAI GF DF V

This Thai classic, reimagined here with zucchini noodles instead of rice noodles, is a versatile dish that can be tailored to satisfy various tastes. Substitute diced chicken, beef strips or peeled shrimp for the tofu, or make it vegan by omitting the eggs.

1¾ cups water

3 tablespoons packed brown sugar

3 tablespoons reduced-sodium tamari or soy sauce

2 tablespoons fresh lime juice

1 tablespoon vegetarian fish sauce or anchovy paste

2 large zucchini

4 tablespoons vegetable oil, divided

1 package (14 ounces) firm tofu, pressed and cut into cubes

2 eggs, lightly beaten

2 cloves garlic, minced

1 tablespoon paprika

¼ teaspoon ground red pepper (optional)

8 ounces fresh bean sprouts, divided

½ cup coarsely chopped peanuts

4 green onions, cut into 1-inch lengths

Lime wedges (optional)

1. Combine water, brown sugar, tamari, lime juice and fish sauce in small bowl; set aside.

2. Spiral zucchini with thin ribbon blade; cut into desired lengths. Heat 1 tablespoon oil in wok over medium-high heat. Add zucchini; stir-fry 2 to 3 minutes or until crisp-tender. Transfer to large bowl.

3. Heat 1 tablespoon oil in wok over medium-high heat. Add tofu; cook about 5 minutes or until browned on all sides, turning occasionally. Transfer to bowl with zucchini.

4. Heat wok over medium heat about 30 seconds or until hot. Drizzle 1 tablespoon oil into wok and heat 15 seconds. Add eggs and cook 1 minute or just until set on bottom, then scramble until cooked but not dry. Transfer to bowl with zucchini.

5. Drizzle remaining 1 tablespoon oil into wok and heat 15 seconds. Add garlic, paprika and ground red pepper, if desired; cook 30 seconds or until fragrant. Add zucchini, tofu, egg and sauce mixture; stir-fry 3 to 5 minutes or until zucchini is tender and coated with sauce. Add bean sprouts, peanuts and green onions; stir-fry about 1 minute or until onions begin to wilt. Serve immediately with lime wedges, if desired.

Makes 6 servings

Calories 330, **Total Fat** 22g, **Saturated Fat** 3g, **Cholesterol** 65mg, **Sodium** 510mg, **Carbohydrate** 20g, **Dietary Fiber** 3g, **Protein** 18g

ZUCCHINI AND FETA CASSEROLE

This zucchini noodle casserole is gluten-free, but if this isn't a concern for you, feel free to substitute regular all-purpose flour for the gluten-free flour.

4 medium zucchini

1 tablespoon butter

2 eggs, beaten

½ cup grated Parmesan cheese

⅓ cup crumbled feta cheese

2 tablespoons chopped fresh parsley

1 tablespoon chickpea flour, gluten-free all-purpose flour blend or all-purpose flour

2 teaspoons chopped fresh marjoram

Dash hot pepper sauce

Salt and black pepper

1. Preheat oven to 375°F. Spray 2-quart baking dish with nonstick cooking spray.

2. Spiral zucchini with thin ribbon blade; cut into 3-inch lengths. Place zucchini in colander and gently squeeze to remove excess moisture.

3. Melt butter in large skillet over medium heat. Add zucchini; cook and stir until slightly browned. Remove from heat. Stir in eggs, cheeses, parsley, flour, marjoram, hot pepper sauce, salt and black pepper; mix well. Spread in prepared casserole.

4. Bake 35 minutes or until hot and bubbly.

Makes 4 servings

Calories 220, **Total Fat** 14g, **Saturated Fat** 8g, **Cholesterol** 125mg, **Sodium** 430mg, **Carbohydrate** 12g, **Dietary Fiber** 3g, **Protein** 15g

SHRIMP CAPRESE ZOODLES

If you can't find fresh mozzarella pearls, use any fresh mozzarella cut into ¼-inch pieces.

2 large zucchini

1 tablespoon plus 2 teaspoons olive oil, divided

2 cups coarsely chopped grape tomatoes

½ cup reduced-sodium vegetable broth or water

4 tablespoons chopped fresh basil, divided

1 tablespoon balsamic vinegar

2 cloves garlic, minced

¼ teaspoon salt

⅛ teaspoon red pepper flakes

8 ounces medium raw shrimp (with tails on), peeled and deveined

1 cup grape tomatoes, halved

2 ounces fresh mozzarella pearls

1. Spiral zucchini with thin ribbon blade; cut into desired lengths. Heat 1 tablespoon oil in large skillet over medium-high heat. Add zucchini; cook and stir 2 to 3 minutes or until crisp-tender. Transfer to large bowl.

2. Heat remaining 2 teaspoons oil in same skillet over medium heat. Add 2 cups chopped tomatoes, broth, 2 tablespoons basil, vinegar, garlic, salt and red pepper flakes. Cook and stir 10 minutes or until tomatoes begin to soften.

3. Add shrimp and 1 cup halved tomatoes to skillet; cook and stir 5 minutes or until shrimp turn pink and opaque. Add zucchini; cook until heated through.

4. Divide mixture evenly among four bowls. Top evenly with cheese and remaining 2 tablespoons basil.

Makes 4 servings

Calories 200, **Total Fat** 10g, **Saturated Fat** 3g, **Cholesterol** 80mg, **Sodium** 610mg, **Carbohydrate** 14g, **Dietary Fiber** 4g, **Protein** 15g

GINGER ZOODLES WITH SESAME EGG STRIPS GF DF V LC

Sesame seeds are available already toasted, but if you have regular untoasted sesame seeds you can easily toast them yourself. Spread seeds in small skillet. Shake skillet over medium heat 2 minutes or until seeds begin to pop and turn golden.

2 large zucchini

1 tablespoon olive oil

5 egg whites

6 teaspoons teriyaki sauce, divided

3 teaspoons sesame seeds, toasted, divided

1 teaspoon dark sesame oil

½ cup reduced-sodium vegetable broth

1 tablespoon minced fresh ginger

⅓ cup sliced green onions

1. Spiral zucchini with thin ribbon blade; cut into desired lengths. Heat olive oil in large nonstick skillet over medium-high heat. Add zucchini; cook and stir 2 to 3 minutes or until crisp-tender. Transfer to large bowl. Wipe out skillet with paper towels.

2. Beat egg whites, 2 teaspoons teriyaki sauce and 1 teaspoon sesame seeds in large bowl.

3. Heat sesame oil in same skillet over medium heat. Pour egg mixture into skillet; cook 1½ to 2 minutes or until bottom is set. Turn over; cook 30 seconds to 1 minute or until cooked through. Gently slide onto plate; cut into ½-inch strips when cool enough to handle.

4. Add broth, ginger and remaining 4 teaspoons teriyaki sauce to skillet. Bring to a boil over high heat; reduce heat to medium. Add zucchini; mix well. Add omelet strips and green onions; heat through. Sprinkle with remaining 2 teaspoons sesame seeds just before serving.

Makes 4 servings

Calories 130, **Total Fat** 7g, **Saturated Fat** 1g, **Cholesterol** 0mg, **Sodium** 410mg, **Carbohydrate** 10g, **Dietary Fiber** 3g, **Protein** 8g

SPAGHETTI AND BEETS AGLIO E OLIO

Spaghetti and beets make a delicious combination when mixed with olive oil, sautéed garlic and buttery bread crumbs. To save time, you could add the spiraled beets to the spaghetti during the last 5 minutes of cooking instead of cooking them separately. However, this will tint the pasta a bright pink color.

2 medium beets, peeled

8 ounces uncooked spaghetti or thin spaghetti

⅓ cup plus 1 tablespoon olive oil, divided

1 cup fresh Italian or French bread crumbs*

4 cloves garlic, very thinly sliced

¾ teaspoon salt (optional)

½ teaspoon red pepper flakes

½ cup chopped fresh Italian parsley

¾ cup shredded Parmesan cheese, divided

To make fresh bread crumbs, tear 2 ounces bread into pieces; process in food processor until coarse crumbs form.

1. Spiral beets with thin ribbon blade; cut into desired lengths. Spray large nonstick skillet with nonstick cooking spray; heat over medium-high heat. Add beets; cook and stir 8 to 10 minutes or until tender. Transfer to bowl; keep warm.

2. Meanwhile, cook spaghetti according to package directions. Drain and return to saucepan, reserving ½ cup water; keep warm.

3. Heat 1 tablespoon oil in large skillet over medium heat. Add bread crumbs; cook 4 to 5 minutes or until golden brown, stirring frequently. Transfer to small bowl.

4. Combine remaining ⅓ cup oil, garlic, salt, if desired, and red pepper flakes in same skillet; cook over medium heat about 3 minutes or until garlic just begins to brown on edges.

5. Add spaghetti and parsley to skillet; toss to coat with oil mixture. Add some of reserved pasta water to moisten pasta, if desired. Stir in beets, bread crumbs and ½ cup cheese. Top with remaining ¼ cup cheese just before serving.

Makes 6 servings

Calories 400, **Total Fat** 19g, **Saturated Fat** 4g, **Cholesterol** 5mg, **Sodium** 330mg, **Carbohydrate** 45g, **Dietary Fiber** 3g, **Protein** 12g

VEGETARIAN RICE NOODLES

½ cup reduced-sodium soy sauce

⅓ cup sugar

¼ cup fresh lime juice

2 fresh red Thai chiles *or* 1 large jalapeño pepper, finely chopped

8 ounces thin rice noodles (rice vermicelli)

2 medium sweet potatoes (1 pound), peeled

1 jicama (8 ounces), peeled

2 large leeks, white and light green parts only

¼ cup vegetable oil

8 ounces firm tofu, drained and cut into triangles

¼ cup chopped unsalted dry-roasted peanuts

2 tablespoons chopped fresh mint

2 tablespoons chopped fresh cilantro

1. Combine soy sauce, sugar, lime juice and chiles in small bowl until well blended; set aside.

2. Place rice noodles in medium bowl. Cover with hot water; let stand 15 minutes or until soft. Drain well; cut into 3-inch lengths.

3. Meanwhile, spiral sweet potatoes and jicama with thin ribbon blade; cut into desired lengths. Spiral leeks with spiral slicing blade.

4. Heat oil in large skillet over medium-high heat. Add tofu; cook 4 minutes per side or until golden. Remove with slotted spatula to paper towel-lined baking sheet.

5. Add jicama to skillet; stir-fry 5 minutes or until lightly browned. Remove to baking sheet. Stir-fry sweet potatoes in batches until tender and browned; remove to baking sheet. Add leeks; stir-fry 1 minute; remove to baking sheet.

6. Stir soy sauce mixture; add to skillet. Cook and stir until sugar dissolves. Add noodles; toss to coat. Gently stir in tofu, vegetables, peanuts, mint and cilantro.

Makes 8 servings

Calories 310, **Total Fat** 12g, **Saturated Fat** 2g, **Cholesterol** 0mg, **Sodium** 610mg, **Carbohydrate** 46g, **Dietary Fiber** 4g, **Protein** 8g

PASTA WITH ONIONS AND GOAT CHEESE

This easy pasta makes a perfect weeknight dinner; it looks and tastes fancy, but comes together easily. Start the onions caramelizing, and you can do the rest of the prep while they're cooking. As soon as they're done, toss everything together and you're ready to serve.

2 large sweet onions

2 teaspoons olive oil

6 ounces uncooked campanelle, orecchiette or farfalle pasta

1 clove garlic, minced

2 tablespoons dry white wine or vegetable broth

1½ teaspoons chopped fresh sage *or* ½ teaspoon dried sage

½ teaspoon salt

¼ teaspoon black pepper

¾ cup (3 ounces) crumbled goat cheese

¼ cup fat-free (skim) milk

2 tablespoons chopped toasted walnuts

1. Spiral onions with thick ribbon blade; cut into desired lengths.

2. Heat oil in large nonstick skillet over medium heat. Add onions; cook 20 to 25 minutes or until golden and caramelized, stirring occasionally.

3. Meanwhile, cook pasta according to package directions, omitting salt. Drain and return to saucepan; keep warm.

4. Add garlic to onions in skillet; cook about 3 minutes or until softened. Add wine, sage, salt and pepper; cook until liquid has evaporated. Remove from heat. Add pasta, goat cheese and milk; stir until cheese is melted. Sprinkle with walnuts.

Makes 4 servings

Calories 300, **Total Fat** 10g, **Saturated Fat** 2g, **Cholesterol** 18mg, **Sodium** 214mg, **Carbohydrate** 42g, **Dietary Fiber** 4g, **Protein** 10g

ZOODLES IN TOMATO SAUCE

Lighten up traditional spaghetti with marinara by substituting zucchini noodles for the pasta. For a more substantial dish, cook 4 ounces dried whole wheat or gluten-free spaghetti according to package directions and combine it with the zucchini before topping with the sauce in step 2.

3 teaspoons olive oil, divided

2 cloves garlic

1 tablespoon tomato paste

1 can (28 ounces) whole tomatoes, undrained

1 teaspoon dried oregano

½ teaspoon salt

2 large zucchini (about 16 ounces each)

¼ cup shredded Parmesan cheese

1. Heat 2 teaspoons oil in medium saucepan over medium heat. Add garlic; cook 1 minute or until fragrant but not browned. Stir in tomato paste; cook 30 seconds, stirring constantly. Add tomatoes with juice, oregano and salt; break up tomatoes with wooden spoon. Bring to a simmer. Reduce heat; cook 30 minutes or until thickened.

2. Meanwhile, spiral zucchini with thin ribbon blade. Heat remaining 1 teaspoon oil in large saucepan over medium-high heat. Add zucchini; cook 4 to 5 minutes or until tender, stirring frequently. Transfer to serving plates; top with tomato sauce and cheese.

Makes 4 servings

Calories 140, **Total Fat** 5g, **Saturated Fat** 2g, **Cholesterol** 5mg, **Sodium** 720mg, **Carbohydrate** 17g, **Dietary Fiber** 6g, **Protein** 7g

VEGETABLE PASTA SAUCE

Slow cookers can be quite handy, especially when making pasta sauce, but if you don't have one (or the time to wait), you can make this sauce on the stove. Spray a large saucepan with cooking spray and heat over medium-high heat. Add the bell peppers, squash, zucchini, mushrooms and garlic; cook and stir 10 minutes or until softened. Add the remaining ingredients and bring to a boil. Reduce the heat to medium-low, cover and simmer 30 minutes to 1 hour or until vegetables are soft and flavors are blended.

1 red bell pepper

1 green bell pepper

1 small yellow squash

1 small zucchini

2 cans (about 14 ounces each) diced tomatoes

1 can (about 14 ounces) no-salt-added whole tomatoes, undrained

1½ cups sliced mushrooms

1 can (6 ounces) tomato paste

4 green onions, chopped

2 tablespoons dried Italian seasoning

1 tablespoon chopped fresh parsley

3 cloves garlic, minced

1 teaspoon salt

1 teaspoon red pepper flakes (optional)

1 teaspoon black pepper

8 ounces uncooked whole wheat or gluten-free pasta

Fresh basil (optional)

1. Spiral bell peppers with spiral slicing blade; cut into desired lengths. Spiral squash and zucchini with spiral slicing blade; stand on cutting board and cut in half to make slices.

2. Combine bell peppers, squash, zucchini, diced tomatoes, whole tomatoes with juice, mushrooms, tomato paste, green onions, Italian seasoning, parsley, garlic, salt, red pepper flakes and black pepper in slow cooker; mix well.

3. Cover; cook on LOW 6 to 8 hours.

4. Cook pasta according to package directions. Serve sauce over pasta. Top with fresh basil, if desired.

Makes 4 servings

....

Calories 370, **Total Fat** 2g, **Saturated Fat** 0g, **Cholesterol** 0mg, **Sodium** 920mg, **Carbohydrate** 79g, **Dietary Fiber** 16g, **Protein** 15g

....

GREEK CHICKEN AND ZOODLES

- 2 large zucchini
- 1 red bell pepper
- 1 tablespoon plus 2 teaspoons olive oil, divided
- 1 jar (6 ounces) marinated artichoke hearts
- 3 cloves garlic, minced
- 1 pound boneless skinless chicken breasts, cut into bite-size pieces
- 1 tablespoon plus 1 teaspoon fresh lemon juice
- 2 teaspoons dried oregano
- 1 teaspoon grated lemon peel
- ¼ to ½ teaspoon dried mint (optional)
- ¼ teaspoon black pepper
- ⅓ cup sliced pitted black olives
- ¼ cup (1 ounce) crumbled feta cheese

1. Spiral zucchini with thin ribbon blade; cut into desired lengths. Spiral bell pepper with spiral slicing blade; cut into desired lengths.

2. Heat 1 tablespoon oil in large nonstick skillet over medium-high heat. Add zucchini; cook and stir 2 to 3 minutes or until crisp-tender. Transfer to large bowl.

3. Drain artichoke hearts, reserving marinade. Cut artichoke hearts into quarters; set aside.

4. Lightly coat same skillet with nonstick cooking spray; heat over medium heat. Add bell pepper and garlic; cook and stir until tender. Transfer to bowl with zucchini.

5. Heat remaining 2 teaspoons oil in same skillet. Add chicken; cook and stir 2 to 3 minutes or until chicken is nearly cooked through.

6. Return vegetables to skillet. Add reserved artichoke marinade, lemon juice, oregano, lemon peel, mint, if desired, and black pepper to skillet; bring to a boil. Reduce heat; simmer, uncovered, 1 to 2 minutes or until chicken is no longer pink. Stir in artichoke hearts and olives. Sprinkle with feta cheese.

Makes 4 servings

......

Calories 300, **Total Fat** 13g, **Saturated Fat** 3g, **Cholesterol** 90mg, **Sodium** 480mg, **Carbohydrate** 15g, **Dietary Fiber** 4g, **Protein** 31g

......

SPINACH FETTUCCINE WITH GARLIC-ONION SAUCE Ⓥ Ⓛ Ⓢ

You can replace regular noodles with zucchini noodles in many recipes, and this one is no exception. If you want to swap zucchini for the pasta, replace the fresh spinach fettuccine with two large zucchini and follow steps 1 and 2 of the previous recipe on page 113.

1 pound Vidalia or other sweet onions

¼ cup (½ stick) butter

1 tablespoon olive oil

12 cloves garlic, chopped

1 tablespoon honey

1 pound fresh spinach fettuccine

¼ cup Marsala wine

Salt and black pepper

Grated Parmesan cheese (optional)

1. Spiral onions with spiral slicing blade; cut into desired lengths.

2. Heat butter and oil in large skillet over medium heat. Add onions and garlic; cover and cook until soft. Add honey; reduce heat to low. Cook, uncovered, 30 minutes, stirring occasionally.

3. Meanwhile, cook pasta according to package directions. Drain and return to saucepan; keep warm.

4. Add wine to onion sauce; cook 5 to 10 minutes or until most of liquid is absorbed. Season to taste with salt and pepper. Pour sauce over pasta; toss to coat. Sprinkle with Parmesan cheese, if desired; serve immediately.

Makes 6 servings

Calories 430, **Total Fat** 12g, **Saturated Fat** 6g, **Cholesterol** 20mg, **Sodium** 90mg, **Carbohydrate** 68g, **Dietary Fiber** 4g, **Protein** 12g

BEET NOODLES WITH EDAMAME, SPINACH AND FETA GF V LC HF

The contrast between red and golden beets makes a striking presentation, but you can make this recipe with all golden or all red beets. In step 2, cook all the beets together instead of cooking them in batches.

4 medium beets (two *each* red and golden)

1 onion

2 tablespoons olive oil, divided

1 cup frozen shelled edamame

¾ cup water

¾ teaspoon dried herbes de Provence

¼ teaspoon salt

⅛ teaspoon black pepper

6 ounces fresh spinach (about 8 cups), torn into small pieces and rinsed

¾ cup (3 ounces) crumbled reduced-fat feta cheese

1. Spiral beets and onion with thin ribbon blade; cut into desired lengths.

2. Heat ½ tablespoon oil in large skillet over medium heat. Add golden beets; cook and stir 7 to 10 minutes or until tender. Transfer to large bowl. Repeat with ½ tablespoon oil and red beets; transfer to separate bowl.

3. Heat remaining 1 tablespoon oil in same skillet. Add onion; cook and stir 4 minutes or until lightly browned. Stir in edamame, water, herbes de Provence, salt and pepper. Reduce heat; cover and simmer 7 minutes.

4. Add spinach with water clinging to leaves; cover and cook 8 minutes or until spinach is tender. Add to beets; mix well. Sprinkle with feta just before serving.

Makes 4 servings

Calories 190, **Total Fat** 11g, **Saturated Fat** 3g, **Cholesterol** 5mg, **Sodium** 690g, **Carbohydrate** 14g, **Dietary Fiber** 5g, **Protein** 10g

FETTUCCINE WITH SHRIMP AND SPIRALED BROCCOLI (HF)

Yes, you can spiral broccoli! Those stems that you generally discard easily transform into ribbons and curlicues with your spiralizer.

1 large head broccoli, florets removed and stem peeled

8 ounces uncooked fettuccine

½ cup loosely packed fresh basil

5 tablespoons shredded Parmesan cheese, divided

2 tablespoons chopped walnuts, toasted

1½ tablespoons extra virgin olive oil

2 cloves garlic, crushed, divided

⅛ teaspoon salt

6 ounces medium cooked shrimp, peeled and deveined

¼ teaspoon black pepper

1 package (6 ounces) fresh baby spinach

1 cup halved grape tomatoes

1. Spiral broccoli stem with thin ribbon blade.

2. Bring large saucepan of water to a boil. Add broccoli florets; cook 3 minutes or until tender. Remove to small bowl using slotted spoon; return water to a boil.

3. Add pasta to water; cook 9 to 11 minutes or until tender, adding spiraled broccoli stem during last minute of cooking. Drain and return to saucepan; keep warm.

4. Combine broccoli, basil, 3 tablespoons cheese, walnuts, 1 tablespoon oil, 1 clove garlic and salt in food processor or blender; process until smooth. Stir into pasta in saucepan; toss to coat. Keep warm.

5. Heat remaining 1½ teaspoons oil in large skillet over medium heat. Add shrimp, remaining 1 clove garlic and pepper; cook until heated through. Stir in spinach and tomatoes; cook until spinach is wilted and tomatoes begin to soften. Stir into pasta. Sprinkle with remaining 2 tablespoons cheese just before serving.

Makes 4 servings

Calories 400, **Total Fat** 14g, **Saturated Fat** 3g, **Cholesterol** 60mg, **Sodium** 470mg, **Carbohydrate** 50g, **Dietary Fiber** 6g, **Protein** 19g

---

SOBA STIR-FRY

8 ounces uncooked soba noodles

1 red bell pepper

½ head napa cabbage

1 tablespoon olive oil

2 cups sliced shiitake mushrooms

2 whole dried red chiles *or* ¼ teaspoon red pepper flakes

1 clove garlic, minced

½ cup reduced-sodium vegetable broth

2 tablespoons reduced-sodium tamari or soy sauce

1 tablespoon rice wine or dry sherry

2 teaspoons cornstarch

1 package (14 ounces) firm tofu, drained and cut into 1-inch cubes

2 green onions, thinly sliced

1. Cook noodles according to package directions. Drain and return to saucepan; keep warm.

2. Spiral bell pepper and cabbage with spiral slicing blade; cut into desired lengths.

3. Heat oil in large nonstick skillet or wok over medium-high heat. Add mushrooms, bell pepper, dried chiles and garlic; cook and stir 3 minutes or until mushrooms are tender. Add cabbage; cover and cook 2 minutes or until cabbage is wilted.

4. Whisk broth, tamari and rice wine into cornstarch in small bowl until smooth. Stir sauce into vegetable mixture. Cook 2 minutes or until sauce is thickened.

5. Stir in tofu and noodles; toss gently until heated through. Sprinkle with green onions. Serve immediately.

Makes 4 servings

Calories 443, **Total Fat** 13g, **Saturated Fat** 2g, **Cholesterol** 0mg, **Sodium** 773mg, **Carbohydrate** 64g, **Dietary Fiber** 6g, **Protein** 27g

ZOODLES WITH SUN-DRIED TOMATO PESTO (GF) (V) (LC) (LS)

This pesto makes a good sandwich spread, topping for grilled meats or dressing for a pasta salad. Make a double batch and store the extra sauce in an airtight container in the refrigerator up to three weeks.

2 large zucchini

3 tablespoons olive oil, divided

½ cup sun-dried tomatoes (not packed in oil)

½ cup hot water

½ cup loosely packed fresh basil leaves

1½ tablespoons grated Parmesan cheese

1 teaspoon dried oregano

1 clove garlic, minced

1. Spiral zucchini with thin ribbon blade; cut into desired lengths.

2. Heat 1 tablespoon oil in large skillet over medium-high heat. Add zucchini; cook and stir 2 to 3 minutes or until crisp-tender. Transfer to large bowl.

3. Combine sun-dried tomatoes and hot water in small bowl; soak 5 minutes or until tomatoes are softened. Drain; reserve liquid.

4. Combine tomatoes, basil, remaining 2 tablespoons oil, cheese, oregano and garlic in food processor or blender. With motor running, add enough reserved liquid through feed tube until mixture is smooth and desired thickness. Spoon over zucchini; toss to coat.

Makes 4 servings

Calories 180, **Total Fat** 12g, **Saturated Fat** 3g, **Cholesterol** 5mg, **Sodium** 85mg, **Carbohydrate** 15g, **Dietary Fiber** 3g, **Protein** 5g

RICE NOODLES WITH BROCCOLI AND TOFU (GF) (V) (V+) (HF)

1 package (14 ounces) firm or extra firm tofu, drained

1 package (8 to 10 ounces) wide rice noodles

3 medium shallots

1 large head broccoli, floret removed and stem peeled

2 tablespoons peanut oil

6 cloves garlic, minced

1 jalapeño pepper, minced

2 teaspoons minced fresh ginger

3 tablespoons reduced-sodium soy sauce

1 tablespoon sweet soy sauce*

1 to 2 tablespoons vegetarian fish sauce, fresh lime juice or regular fish sauce

Fresh basil leaves (optional)

*If sweet soy sauce is not available, substitute 1 tablespoon soy sauce plus 1 tablespoon packed brown sugar.

1. Cut tofu crosswise into two pieces. Place tofu on cutting board between layers of paper towels; place weighted saucepan or baking dish on top of tofu. Let stand 30 minutes to drain. Place rice noodles in large bowl; cover with boiling water. Soak 30 minutes or until soft.

2. Spiral shallots with spiral slicing blade. Spiral broccoli stem with thin ribbon blade.

3. Cut tofu into bite-size squares and blot dry. Heat oil in large skillet or wok over high heat. Add tofu; cook about 5 minutes or until tofu is lightly browned on all sides, turning occasionally. Transfer to bowl.

4. Add shallots, garlic, jalapeño pepper and ginger to skillet. Stir-fry 2 to 3 minutes. Add broccol florets and stems; stir-fry 1 minute. Cover and cook 3 minutes or until broccoli is crisp-tender.

5. Drain noodles; add to skillet and stir to combine. Return tofu to skillet; add soy sauces and fish sauce. Stir-fry about 8 minutes or until noodles are coated and flavors are blended. Garnish with basil.

Makes 4 servings

Calories 450, **Total Fat** 14g, **Saturated Fat** 2g, **Cholesterol** 0mg, **Sodium** 990mg, **Carbohydrate** 64g, **Dietary Fiber** 5g, **Protein** 6g

PASTA PRIMAVERA WITH RICOTTA

6 ounces uncooked fettuccine

1 cup reduced-fat ricotta cheese

½ cup low-fat (1%) milk

1 zucchini

1 yellow squash

1 red bell pepper

4 teaspoons olive oil

1 clove garlic, minced

½ teaspoon red pepper flakes

1 cup fresh or frozen peas

½ teaspoon salt

1 teaspoon dried Italian seasoning

½ cup freshly grated Parmesan cheese

1. Cook fettuccine according to package directions. Drain and return to saucepan; keep warm. Whisk ricotta and milk in small bowl.

2. Spiral zucchini and yellow squash with thin ribbon blade. Spiral bell pepper with spiral slicing blade. Cut vegetables into desired lengths.

3. Heat oil in large nonstick skillet over medium heat. Add garlic and red pepper flakes; cook and stir 1 minute. Add yellow squash, zucchini, bell pepper, peas, salt and Italian seasoning; cook and stir 5 minutes or until vegetables are crisp-tender.

4. Combine fettuccine, vegetables and ricotta mixture in large bowl; mix gently until well blended. Sprinkle with Parmesan cheese just before serving.

Makes 4 servings

Calories 420, **Total Fat** 15g, **Saturated Fat** 7g, **Cholesterol** 40mg, **Sodium** 700mg, **Carbohydrate** 54g, **Dietary Fiber** 6g, **Protein** 22g

Side Dishes

HONEYED BEETS GF V LC LS

Sweet, earthy beets are glazed with a tangy, sweet glaze in this easy side dish. If you can't find golden beets, or don't want to deal with red beets, use two beets of the same color.

1 medium red beet (8 ounces)

1 medium golden beet (8 ounces)

1 tablespoon vegetable oil

¼ cup unsweetened apple juice

2 tablespoons cider vinegar

1 tablespoon honey

2 teaspoons cornstarch

Salt and black pepper

1. Preheat oven to 425°F. Line baking sheet with parchment paper.

2. Spiral beets with thin ribbon blade; cut into desired lengths. Spread on prepared baking sheet, keeping golden beets separate from red beets; drizzle with oil. Bake 15 minutes or until tender, stirring occasionally.

3. Combine apple juice, vinegar, honey and cornstarch in large nonstick skillet. Cook over medium heat until shimmering, stirring occasionally. Stir in beets; season to taste with salt and pepper. Simmer 3 minutes or until beets are glazed.

Makes 4 servings

Calories 90, **Total Fat** 4g, **Saturated Fat** 0g, **Cholesterol** 0mg, **Sodium** 60mg, **Carbohydrate** 15g, **Dietary Fiber** 2g, **Protein** 1g

MEDITERRANEAN VEGETABLE BAKE

This casserole makes a tasty side dish with roasted chicken or grilled lamb or beef. To make it a vegetarian entrée, add slices of fresh mozzarella cheese with the eggplant, tomatoes and mushrooms. Serve it with a Greek salad and slices of bread.

1 small red onion

1 medium zucchini

1 yellow squash

2 tomatoes, sliced

1 small eggplant, sliced

1 portobello mushroom, sliced

2 cloves garlic, finely chopped

3 tablespoons olive oil

2 teaspoons chopped fresh rosemary

⅔ cup dry white wine

Salt and black pepper

1. Preheat oven to 350°F. Grease 13×9-inch baking dish.

2. Spiral red onion, zucchini and yellow squash with thick ribbon blade. Arrange tomatoes, eggplant and mushroom alternately in prepared baking dish; top with spiraled vegetables and sprinkle evenly with garlic. Combine oil and rosemary in small bowl; drizzle over vegetables. Pour wine over vegetables; season with salt and pepper. Cover loosely with foil.

3. Bake 20 minutes. Uncover; bake 10 to 15 minutes or until vegetables are tender.

Makes 4 to 6 servings

Calories 230, **Total Fat** 2g, **Saturated Fat** 0g, **Cholesterol** 0mg, **Sodium** 20mg, **Carbohydrate** 25g, **Dietary Fiber** 5g, **Protein** 4g

SPANISH RICE-STYLE RUTABAGA WITH AVOCADO : GF DF V V+ HF

Serve this Spanish rice-inspired side as a healthier alternative to Spanish rice. Try it alongside grilled meats, or stuffed into tacos, burritos or bell peppers. For a heartier variation, stir in some cooked black beans and chopped cilantro.

1 large rutabaga, peeled

1 onion

2 tablespoons olive oil

1 clove garlic, minced

½ teaspoon salt

½ teaspoon dried oregano

½ teaspoon ground cumin

½ teaspoon ground turmeric

1 can (about 14 ounces) reduced-sodium vegetable broth

1 avocado, diced

1. Spiral rutabaga with thick ribbon blade. Place in food processor; pulse until small pieces form. Spiral onion with thin ribbon blade; cut into desired lengths.

2. Heat oil in medium saucepan over medium heat. Add onion and garlic; cook and stir until onion is tender. Add rutabaga, salt, oregano, cumin, turmeric and broth; bring to a boil. Reduce heat; cover and cook 10 minutes or until rutabaga is tender. Remove from heat; stir in avocado.

Makes 4 to 6 servings

....

Calories 230, **Total Fat** 14g, **Saturated Fat** 2g, **Cholesterol** 0mg, **Sodium** 380mg, **Carbohydrate** 26g, **Dietary Fiber** 9g, **Protein** 3g

....

SKILLET ROASTED ROOT VEGETABLES GF DF V HF

Think beyond dinner and try these tasty roasted vegetables as a side with eggs at breakfast instead of hash browns, or with sandwiches at lunch instead of potato chips.

1 sweet potato, peeled
2 parsnips
1 large red onion
2 large carrots
1 turnip, peeled
3 tablespoons olive oil
2 tablespoons honey or agave nectar
2 tablespoons balsamic vinegar
1 teaspoon coarse salt
1 teaspoon dried thyme
¼ teaspoon ground red pepper
¼ teaspoon black pepper

1. Preheat oven to 400°F.

2. Spiral sweet potato, parsnips, onion, carrots and turnip with thick ribbon blade; place in medium bowl. Add oil, honey, vinegar, salt, thyme, ground red pepper and black pepper; toss to coat. Spread vegetables in single layer in large (12-inch) cast iron skillet.

3. Roast 30 to 45 minutes or until vegetables are tender, stirring once halfway through cooking time.

Makes 4 servings

Calories 240, **Total Fat** 11g, **Saturated Fat** 2g, **Cholesterol** 0mg, **Sodium** 550mg, **Carbohydrate** 36g, **Dietary Fiber** 6g, **Protein** 2g

---

APPLE-CARROT CASSEROLE (V) (HF)

Look for extra large carrots (1½ inches in diameter at least) for this recipe. It is much easier to spiral large carrots, and they make prettier spirals.

6 large carrots (about 1½ inches in diameter)

4 large Granny Smith apples, peeled

¼ cup all-purpose flour

1 tablespoon packed brown sugar

½ teaspoon salt

½ teaspoon ground nutmeg

1 tablespoon cold unsalted butter, cut into pieces

½ cup orange juice

1. Preheat oven to 350°F. Spiral carrots and apples with thick ribbon blade. Layer in 2-quart baking dish.

2. Combine flour, brown sugar, salt and nutmeg in small bowl; cut in butter. Sprinkle over casserole and drizzle orange juice over topping.

3. Bake 30 minutes or until carrots and apples are tender.

Makes 6 servings

Calories 170, **Total Fat** 3g, **Saturated Fat** 2g, **Cholesterol** 5mg, **Sodium** 240mg, **Carbohydrate** 35g, **Dietary Fiber** 6g, **Protein** 2g

POTATO AND LEEK GRATIN Ⓥ

2 large leeks

2 pounds baking potatoes, peeled (about 4 medium)

3 tablespoons unsalted butter, divided

2 tablespoons minced garlic

2 cups reduced-fat (2%) milk

3 eggs

1 teaspoon salt

¼ teaspoon white pepper

2 to 3 slices dense day-old white bread, such as French or Italian

¼ cup grated Parmesan cheese

1. Preheat oven to 375°F. Spray shallow 2½-quart baking dish with nonstick cooking spray.

2. Spiral leeks with spiral slicing blade; cut into desired lengths. Spiral potatoes with spiral slicing blade; stand on cutting board and cut in half to make slices.

3. Melt 1 tablespoon butter in large skillet over medium heat. Add leeks and garlic; cook and stir 8 to 10 minutes or until leeks are softened. Remove from heat.

4. Layer half of potato slices in prepared baking dish; top with half of leek mixture. Repeat layers. Whisk milk, eggs, salt and pepper in medium bowl until well blended; pour evenly over vegetables.

5. Tear bread slices into 1-inch pieces. Place in food processor; process until fine crumbs form. Measure ¾ cup crumbs; place in small bowl. Melt remaining 2 tablespoons butter; stir into crumb mixture. Sprinkle evenly over vegetables.

6. Bake about 1 hour 15 minutes or until top is golden brown and potatoes are tender. Let stand 5 to 10 minutes before serving.

Makes 8 servings

Calories 250, **Total Fat** 9g, **Saturated Fat** 5g, **Cholesterol** 90mg, **Sodium** 460mg, **Carbohydrate** 34g, **Dietary Fiber** 3g, **Protein** 10g

ROASTED CURLY CARROTS, POTATOES AND ONIONS GF DF V V+

These simple roasted vegetables make a perfect snack or healthy alternative to potato chips or French fries. They're also a fun sharable snack for parties; just double or triple the recipe and bake on additional baking sheets.

2 large carrots
  (4 ounces)

1 yellow onion
  (4 ounces)

1 medium red potato
  (4 ounces)

1 tablespoon dark
  sesame oil

½ teaspoon dried
  thyme

¼ teaspoon salt

¼ teaspoon black
  pepper

1. Preheat oven to 425°F. Line baking sheet with parchment paper or spray with nonstick cooking spray.

2. Spiral carrots and onion with thin ribbon blade and spiral potato with thick ribbon blade; cut vegetables into desired lengths. Spread on prepared baking sheet. Drizzle with sesame oil and sprinkle with thyme, salt and pepper; toss to coat. Arrange in single layer.

3. Bake 15 to 17 minutes or until vegetables are beginning to brown on edges, stirring occasionally.

Makes 2 servings

Calories 145, **Total Fat** 7g, **Saturated Fat** 1g, **Cholesterol** 0mg, **Sodium** 331mg, **Carbohydrate** 19g, **Dietary Fiber** 3g, **Protein** 2g

ZUCCHINI AND SWEET POTATO STUFFED PEPPERS GF DF V V+ LS HF

Sweet potatoes replace rice in these savory stuffed peppers. If you don't want to get out the food processor to make rice-size pieces of sweet potato, simply coarsely chop the sweet potato instead. In step 4, sauté it for a few minutes before adding the other vegetables and seasonings.

4 red bell peppers

1 medium zucchini (8 ounces)

1 small onion

1 sweet potato, peeled

2 teaspoons olive oil

½ cup diced celery

¾ teaspoon dried Italian seasoning

½ teaspoon salt

¼ teaspoon black pepper

¼ cup vegetable broth

2 tablespoons toasted pine nuts*

To toast pine nuts, spread in single layer in heavy skillet. Cook over medium heat 1 to 2 minutes or until nuts are lightly browned, stirring frequently.

1. Preheat oven to 375°F. Spray baking dish with nonstick cooking spray.

2. Slice tops off bell peppers; remove seeds and membranes. Bring large pot of water to a boil. Add bell peppers; cover and cook 5 minutes or until bell peppers start to soften. Remove with tongs; drain upside down.

3. Spiral zucchini and onion with thick ribbon blade; cut into desired lengths. Spiral sweet potato with thin ribbon blade; place in food processor. Pulse until sweet potato forms small pieces.

4. Heat oil in large skillet over medium-high heat. Add zucchini, onion, celery, Italian seasoning, salt and black pepper; cook 5 to 7 minutes or until zucchini is browned and vegetables are tender, stirring occasionally. Add sweet potato during last 3 minutes of cooking; reduce heat if browning too quickly.

5. Remove from heat. Stir in broth and pine nuts; spoon into bell peppers. Transfer to prepared baking dish. Bake 15 minutes or until sweet potatoes are tender and filling is heated through.

Makes 4 servings

Calories 140, **Total Fat** 6g, **Saturated Fat** 1g, **Cholesterol** 0mg, **Sodium** 100mg, **Carbohydrate** 21g, **Dietary Fiber** 6g, **Protein** 4g

SPIRALED RATATOUILLE (GF) (DF) (V) (V+) (LC) (LS)

This classic Provençal dish gets an update with spiralized onions, squash and bell pepper. Serve it hot, cold or room temperature as a side dish or appetizer.

1 onion

1 yellow squash

1 green bell pepper

2 teaspoons olive oil

2 cloves garlic, minced

4 cups cubed unpeeled eggplant

1 cup chopped fresh tomatoes

¼ cup finely chopped fresh basil *or* 1 teaspoon dried basil

1 tablespoon finely chopped fresh oregano *or* 1 teaspoon dried oregano

2 teaspoons finely chopped fresh thyme *or* ½ teaspoon dried thyme

1. Spiral onion and yellow squash with thick ribbon blade and spiral bell pepper with spiral slicing blade. Cut vegetables into desired lengths.

2. Heat oil in large skillet over medium heat. Add onion, bell pepper and garlic; cook and stir 5 minutes or until tender. Add eggplant, yellow squash, tomatoes, basil, oregano and thyme. Cover and cook 8 to 10 minutes or until vegetables are tender. Uncover; cook 2 to 3 minutes or until all liquid is absorbed.

Makes 4 servings

Calories 31, **Total Fat** 1g, **Saturated Fat** 1g, **Cholesterol** 0mg, **Sodium** 5mg, **Carbohydrate** 7g, **Dietary Fiber** 2g, **Protein** 1g

Desserts

PEAR SPICE CAKE (DF) (V) (V+)

This cake uses ground flaxseed and water as an egg replacer to make it vegan. If this is not a concern, you can substitute 2 eggs for the flaxseed and 6 tablespoons water.

4 pears, peeled

2 cups granulated sugar

½ cup chopped walnuts (optional)

6 tablespoons water

2 tablespoons ground flaxseed

3 cups all-purpose flour

2 teaspoons baking soda

¾ teaspoon ground cinnamon

½ teaspoon salt

¼ teaspoon ground nutmeg

⅛ teaspoon ground cloves

1 cup vegetable oil

1½ teaspoons vanilla

Powdered sugar (optional)

1. Spiral pears with spiral slicing blade. Stand on cutting board and cut in half to make slices.

2. Combine pears, granulated sugar and walnuts, if desired, in medium bowl; mix lightly. Let stand 1 hour, stirring occasionally.

3. Combine water and flaxseed in small saucepan; simmer over medium-low heat 5 minutes. Cool to room temperature.

4. Preheat oven to 375°F. Grease and flour 10-inch tube pan.

5. Combine flour, baking soda, cinnamon, salt, nutmeg and cloves in medium bowl.

6. Whisk flaxseed mixture, oil and vanilla in large bowl. Add flour mixture; mix well. Add pear mixture; mix well. Pour into prepared pan.

7. Bake 1 hour 10 minutes or until toothpick inserted near center comes out clean. Cool in pan 20 minutes. Loosen edges and remove to rack to cool completely. Sprinkle with powdered sugar just before serving, if desired.

Makes 12 servings

Calories 450, **Total Fat** 19g, **Saturated Fat** 2g, **Cholesterol** 0mg, **Sodium** 310mg, **Carbohydrate** 67g, **Dietary Fiber** 3g, **Protein** 4g

RUSTIC APPLE CROUSTADE ⓥ Ⓛ Ⓢ

For this simple croustade, try Honeycrisp, Granny Smith, Fuji or Jonathan apples, or a combination.

1⅓ cups all-purpose flour

¼ teaspoon salt

2 tablespoons unsalted butter

2 tablespoons shortening

4 to 5 tablespoons ice water

3 large apples

⅓ cup packed light brown sugar

1 tablespoon cornstarch

1 teaspoon ground cinnamon, divided

1 egg white, beaten

1 tablespoon granulated sugar

1. Combine flour and salt in small bowl. Cut in butter and shortening with pastry blender until mixture resembles coarse crumbs. Stir in ice water, 1 tablespoon at a time, until mixture comes together and forms soft dough. Wrap in plastic wrap; refrigerate 30 minutes.

2. Preheat oven to 375°F. Line baking sheet with parchment paper. Roll out pastry on floured surface to ⅛-inch thickness; cut into 12-inch circle. Transfer to prepared baking sheet. Refrigerate until ready to serve.

3. Spiral apples with spiral slicing blade; stand on cutting board and cut in half to make slices.

4. Combine brown sugar, cornstarch and ¾ teaspoon cinnamon in medium bowl; mix well. Add apples; toss well. Spoon apple mixture into center of pastry, leaving 1½-inch border. Bring pastry over apples, folding edges in gently and pressing down lightly. Brush egg white over pastry. Combine remaining ¼ teaspoon cinnamon and granulated sugar in small bowl; sprinkle evenly over apples and crust.

5. Bake 35 to 40 minutes or until apples are tender and crust is golden brown. Let stand 20 minutes before serving. Cut into wedges.

Makes 8 servings

Calories 213, **Total Fat** 6g, **Saturated Fat** 1g, **Cholesterol** 0mg, **Sodium** 118mg, **Carbohydrate** 37g, **Dietary Fiber** 3g, **Protein** 3g

AUTUMN FRUIT CRISP DF V V+ LS

2 large apples, peeled

1 pear, peeled

⅓ cup old-fashioned oats

¼ cup packed brown sugar

2 tablespoons whole wheat flour

½ teaspoon ground cinnamon

2 tablespoons cold dairy-free margarine or butter, cut into small pieces

1. Preheat oven to 350°F. Spray 8-inch square baking dish with nonstick cooking spray.

2. Spiral apples and pear with spiral slicing blade; stand on cutting board and cut in half to make slices.

3. Combine apples and pear in prepared baking dish. Combine oats, brown sugar, flour and cinnamon in medium bowl; mix well. Cut in margarine with pastry blender or two knives until mixture resembles coarse crumbs. Sprinkle evenly over fruit mixture.

4. Bake 35 to 40 minutes or until fruit is tender and topping is lightly browned.

Makes 6 servings

Calories 134, **Total Fat** 4g, **Saturated Fat** 3g, **Cholesterol** 10mg, **Sodium** 32mg, **Carbohydrate** 24g, **Dietary Fiber** 3g, **Protein** 1g

SWEDISH APPLE PIE Ⓥ Ⓛ🅢

This delicious pie is more like a crisp (it doesn't use pie crust) and comes together in a snap. As the topping bakes, it forms a crispy shell that perfectly complements the softened cinnamon-sugar apples.

4 Granny Smith apples, peeled

1 cup plus 1 tablespoon sugar, divided

1 tablespoon ground cinnamon

½ cup (1 stick) butter, melted

1 cup all-purpose flour

1 egg

½ cup coarsely chopped nuts (optional)

1. Preheat oven to 350°F.

2. Spiral apples with spiral slicing blade; stand on cutting board and cut in half to make slices. Spread apples in deep-dish 9-inch pie plate.

3. Combine 1 tablespoon sugar and cinnamon in small bowl. Sprinkle over apples. Drizzle butter over apples.

4. Combine remaining 1 cup sugar, flour, egg and nuts, if desired, in medium bowl. (Mixture will be thick.) Sprinkle over apples. Bake 50 to 55 minutes or until topping is golden brown.

Makes 8 servings

Calories 340, **Total Fat** 12g, **Saturated Fat** 7g, **Cholesterol** 55mg, **Sodium** 10mg, **Carbohydrate** 57g, **Dietary Fiber** 3g, **Protein** 3g

CINNAMON PEAR CRISP DF V V+ LS

8 pears, peeled

¾ cup unsweetened apple juice concentrate

½ cup golden raisins

¼ cup plus 3 tablespoons all-purpose flour, divided

1 teaspoon ground cinnamon

⅓ cup quick oats

3 tablespoons packed dark brown sugar

3 tablespoons dairy-free margarine, melted

1. Preheat oven to 375°F. Spray 11×7-inch baking dish with nonstick cooking spray.

2. Spiral pears with spiral slicing blade; stand on cutting board and cut in half to make slices.

3. Combine pears, apple juice concentrate, raisins, 3 tablespoons flour and cinnamon in large bowl; mix well. Transfer to prepared baking dish.

4. Combine oats, remaining ¼ cup flour, brown sugar and margarine in medium bowl; stir until mixture resembles coarse crumbs. Sprinkle evenly over pear mixture.

5. Bake 1 hour or until topping is golden brown.

Makes 12 servings

Calories 179, **Total Fat** 4g, **Saturated Fat** 1g, **Cholesterol** 0mg, **Sodium** 40mg, **Carbohydrate** 38g, **Dietary Fiber** 3g, **Protein** 2g

Metric Conversion Chart

VOLUME MEASUREMENTS (dry)

1/8 teaspoon = 0.5 mL
1/4 teaspoon = 1 mL
1/2 teaspoon = 2 mL
3/4 teaspoon = 4 mL
1 teaspoon = 5 mL
1 tablespoon = 15 mL
2 tablespoons = 30 mL
1/4 cup = 60 mL
1/3 cup = 75 mL
1/2 cup = 125 mL
2/3 cup = 150 mL
3/4 cup = 175 mL
1 cup = 250 mL
2 cups = 1 pint = 500 mL
3 cups = 750 mL
4 cups = 1 quart = 1 L

VOLUME MEASUREMENTS (fluid)

1 fluid ounce (2 tablespoons) = 30 mL
4 fluid ounces (1/2 cup) = 125 mL
8 fluid ounces (1 cup) = 250 mL
12 fluid ounces (1 1/2 cups) = 375 mL
16 fluid ounces (2 cups) = 500 mL

WEIGHTS (mass)

1/2 ounce = 15 g
1 ounce = 30 g
3 ounces = 90 g
4 ounces = 120 g
8 ounces = 225 g
10 ounces = 285 g
12 ounces = 360 g
16 ounces = 1 pound = 450 g

DIMENSIONS

1/16 inch = 2 mm
1/8 inch = 3 mm
1/4 inch = 6 mm
1/2 inch = 1.5 cm
3/4 inch = 2 cm
1 inch = 2.5 cm

OVEN TEMPERATURES

250°F = 120°C
275°F = 140°C
300°F = 150°C
325°F = 160°C
350°F = 180°C
375°F = 190°C
400°F = 200°C
425°F = 220°C
450°F = 230°C

BAKING PAN SIZES

Utensil	Size in Inches/Quarts	Metric Volume	Size in Centimeters
Baking or Cake Pan (square or rectangular)	8×8×2	2 L	20×20×5
	9×9×2	2.5 L	23×23×5
	12×8×2	3 L	30×20×5
	13×9×2	3.5 L	33×23×5
Loaf Pan	8×4×3	1.5 L	20×10×7
	9×5×3	2 L	23×13×7
Round Layer Cake Pan	8×1½	1.2 L	20×4
	9×1½	1.5 L	23×4
Pie Plate	8×1¼	750 mL	20×3
	9×1¼	1 L	23×3
Baking Dish or Casserole	1 quart	1 L	—
	1½ quart	1.5 L	—
	2 quart	2 L	—